The Walk on Layton

52 Modern Parables for
Your Journey

JO ANN WALCZAK

Copyright © 2024 Jo Ann Walczak

All rights reserved.

Manufactured in the United States of America

No portion of this book may be reproduced or transmitted in any form whatsoever by any means—electronic, mechanical, photocopy, recording, scanning or other—without the prior written permission of the author and publisher except for brief quotations in critical reviews or articles.

Unless otherwise noted, all scripture is from the New International Version (NIV).

Author's Note: Walk has been capitalized in all instances where it is a noun since it is the major theme of the book. When "walk" is used as a verb, it is in lower case.

Published by Bethel Road Publishing

Cover Design: Robin K. Axtell
Editing/Interior Design: Michele Chynoweth
Photos of Author: Caitlyn Lukasik
Cover photo: Tom and Fran Novitsky

ISBN: 9798218560720

Dedication

Bryan R. and Janine Z. Walczak, Ben, Anna, Claire Walczak
Trevor J. and Casie C. Walczak, Wyatt, Maverick, Kassadee Walczak

To my generations: These personal stories confirm God's faithfulness to us. *"On this day tell your son, I do this because of what the LORD did for me'...."* (Exodus 13:8).

God commanded the Israelites to take an omer of manna and *"keep it for generations to come"* as proof of His faithfulness (Exodus 16:32-33).

This collection of stories represents my omer of manna, proof of His faithfulness for you.

May every one of my generations have an Emmaus Road encounter with Jesus and may the remainder of their days on earth be an obedient, trusting Walk with our Savior on Layton—or wherever they may live.

IN MEMORY OF
Joseph and Annette E. Jones
John O. and Winifred M. Jones
William T. and Ethel H. Evans
Leo and Mary B. Walczak

Table of Contents

TWO ROADS... vii
PREFACE... 1
INTRODUCTION.. 3

PART 1: THE WALK BEGINS

1. Dead End.. 11
2. The Trailhead... 15
3. Walking Alone....................................... 21
4. Cross-Bearing.. 27
5. The Trail Guide..................................... 31

PART 2: BUMPS IN THE ROAD

6. Thieves!... 37
7. What's in a Name?................................. 41
8. Roots to Breathe.................................... 45
9. Refuge in the Rain................................. 49

PART 3: THE PEOPLE WE MEET

10. People Matter....................................... 55
11. Reach Out and Touch........................... 61
12. The Old Dirt Road................................ 65
13. Strangers We See.................................. 71

PART 4: PATHS OF PURPOSE

14. Who's Got Talent?................................ 77
15. Marching in Armor............................... 83
16. Purposeful Paths................................... 87
17. Artists in Kindness............................... 91

PART 5: ENJOY THE SCENERY

18. Winter Magnificat.................................97
19. Day Lilies in Bloom............................. 99
20. We Need Beauty.................................103
21. The Vines and Branches.......................... 107
22. Rest Awhile................................... 111

PART 6: FRIENDS AND FAMILY

23. Dining Table Relationships.......................119
24. Making Memories.................................123
25. Campfire Stories............................... 129
26. Clothes for the Road............................ 133
27. Friendly Faces.................................137
28. Letters Home...................................141

PART 7: AROUND THE WORLD

29. Cultural Bridges.............................. 147
30. A Trail of Breadcrumbs......................... 153
31. Surrounded................................... 157
32. Orphanage Reunion............................ 163
33. Potluck Hot Pot.............................. 167
34. Celebrations................................. 171
35. So Far Away................................. 177
36. Great Adventures............................. 181

PART 8: SHINY DAYS

37. Dance Along the Way........................... 187
38. Simple Joys...................................191
39. Everyday Miracles............................. 195
40. The Best Medicine............................ 199

PART 9: FUTURE GENERATIONS

41. The Narrow Gate.................................... 205
42. Grabbing for Rings............................... 209
43. One-of-a-Kind Life................................ 213
44. Trudging with Excitement...................... 217
45. Shining Like a Star............................... 221

PART 10: THE FINISH LINE

46. Locusts.. 225
47. Tearing Down and Building Up................ 229
48. New Frontiers....................................... 233
49. The Comfort of Song............................. 237
50. The Waiting Room................................ 243
51. The House on Layton............................ 247
52. A Moment in Time................................ 251

ACKNOWLEDGMENTS................................ 253
ABOUT THE AUTHOR................................ 257

Two Roads

Two roads converged in these country woods,
And I,
I walked on Layton Road
Because of the Emmaus Road.

One road—blind to God.
The other road—the way of God,
His presence, His promises, His forgiveness.
One, the way of self-focus; the Other, the way to salvation.

Jesus walked Emmaus beside me, unrecognized.
Jesus, ever present, remained
Long-suffering, vigilant, patient.
He waited
For acknowledgment and acceptance,
As my Savior, Redeemer.

Then, Emmaus intersected with Layton,
And eyes open, I met my Savior.
Choice, change, salvation stood at the crossroads.

Grace, mercy, hope,
Signpost directions of the Layton journey,

THE WALK ON LAYTON

Declared His presence.
Paved with an Emmaus commitment,
Layton changed forever.

Two roads converged in a country wood,
And an ordinary life began an extraordinary Walk.
In step with the Savior,
Movement in tandem,
Hearts entwined,
Home in sight.
I took His road,
And that has made all the difference.

Jo Ann Walczak

Preface

Layton Road climbs a mountain.

For three miles the road ascends gradually, always upward. The trappings of shops, gas stations, and restaurants are absent on Layton, but the presence of forests, farms, fields, and families abound. A cross between suburban and country living, Layton Road is a place for ordinary people. I live on Layton.

The Pennsylvania Department of Transportation recently paved our road, eliminating ruts, cracks, and gaping pits, creating a smooth surface, a joy to travel for its residents. But life on Layton Road has not always been an unruffled, level, easy-to-navigate road. Potholes and ditches have flourished, as rampant as the goldenrods lining the gutters, despite Penn DOT's best efforts.

Layton Road has been home for most of my seventy-plus years and, before me, home to my parents and grandparents for almost one hundred years. Life has been lived from my home-base of Layton and encompasses where I walk through daily life.

Dad was a walker. He kept up a steady walking routine and a hearty pace for most of his ninety-eight years. He walked six days a week and rested on Sunday. He walked for strength, health, and pleasure.

His dad, Grandpa Jones, walked out of necessity. When Grandpa suffered a stroke behind the wheel of his 1950 Chevy and revived as a hood ornament on someone's front porch, Dad insisted Grandpa forfeit the keys to his car and declared his driving days over. For the remainder of his years Grandpa walked—down the mountain five miles to his sister Bessie's in Blakely, to his favorite pub in Olyphant to sing with his buddies, and, on occasion, to friends who lived sixteen miles away in Pittston.

Although my walk wasn't intended for physical health like Dad or out of necessity like Grandpa, it became a metaphor for following along a new pathway with a different focus. Walking Layton Road involved learning how to follow hard after the One who called me His own, how to depend on Him for the challenges and trials of daily life, how to live above circumstances as a child of God, and how to allow my life to be used for His glory—right here on the country road I called home.

Walking with Jesus Christ became the way to live, the path to follow—the challenge. But this Walk wasn't always a concern or a priority. Jesus rarely crossed my mind for the first couple decades. An Emmaus Road Encounter (the original Bible story is recounted in Luke 24:13-35) explains the change in how I walk.

While Layton Road's three miles extend from the town of Chinchilla in Northeastern Pennsylvania to a dead end at St. Joseph's Cemetery in Scott Township, the seven-mile Emmaus Road of the first century BC connected one of the largest cities of its time, Jerusalem, to the village of Emmaus. But the geographical locations of Layton Road and Emmaus Road are not as important as the lessons learned on the journeys along them. One road dead ends at a cemetery. The other leads Home. What begins on an Emmaus Road turns a Walk on Layton Road into a lifetime adventure.

Introduction

THE EMMAUS ROAD ENCOUNTER
(Luke 24:13-35)

"Do you think he's alive?" Isaac asked his friend Cleopas.

"How could he be? We watched him die!" Cleopas said.

"Perhaps he just fainted away, and when they put him in the cool tomb, he revived."

"Don't be ridiculous, Isaac. The women bathed his body. If there was a heartbeat, they would have known."

"Yes, he was truly dead. How could Jesus have survived? The soldier's sword plunged into his side, and he hung there bleeding all afternoon," Isaac said.

"Not to mention the spikes hammered into his hands and feet. I will never be able to erase that picture from my mind."

"Or the humiliation of the ring of two-inch thorns jammed on his head called a crown. Horrible."

Conversation gushed non-stop as the friends walked and talked on the Emmaus Road that Sunday, discussing what might have happened to Jesus' body and remembering the incredible events of the past few months as they had followed him around the countryside. Some of the women in their friend group had been to the tomb that morning and the body was gone. Had someone stolen it?

Cleopas and Isaac, oblivious to their surroundings on the road, talked simultaneously, hands gesturing, voices rising about this headline of the day. Where was Jesus' body? He had been dead for three days. Cleopas and Isaac watched Jesus die—not because they wished to witness their friend's last hours but because they wanted to be close to Him. They yearned to lean into His love and strength as long as possible.

Finally, lost in their own thoughts of sorrow and loss and emotionally spent, the two men stopped talking, each silently rehearsing the terror of Friday's Roman crucifixion of their friend Jesus, the one they had all been convinced was the Messiah.

"Perhaps we were foolish," Cleopas said quietly, hesitant to share his true feelings with Isaac. "If he was the Messiah, they could never have put him through such agony. The power of God would have stepped in to save him, right? Yet how else can we explain the incredible miracles he performed?"

The afternoon sun compounded the weariness, sorrow, and disappointment of the two who had already walked three miles from Jerusalem and had four more to go before they reached the home of Cleopas' family in Emmaus.

Rousing himself from dark remembrances, Isaac's voice choked and dropped to a whisper. "What do you think, Cleopas? Was Jesus really the Messiah? I'd hoped he was the Promised One."

Lost in their thoughts, neither realized a stranger suddenly kept in step beside them on the dusty Emmaus Road. "What's this you are discussing so intently as you walk along, my friends?" the stranger asked. "And why do you both look so downcast? Anyone seeing you both would think you had lost your best friend. It's a beautiful day. Smile. Why are you looking so grim?"

"You must be the only one in all of Jerusalem who does not know what has happened the last few days there." Cleopas shook his head, rolling his eyes at Isaac.

"Fill me in. What has happened?" The stranger walked alongside them with interest.

Eager to recount recent events in Jerusalem, Isaac plunged into the story of Jesus of Nazareth. "This Jesus was truly a man of God, a prophet. He was dynamic in words and works. He was blessed by God and all the people." Warming to his memories, Isaac related stories of lepers healed, the blind made to see, demons cast out by this godly man from Nazareth.

"But," Cleopas broke into Isaac's lecture, "he was killed. The high priests and leaders betrayed him, sentenced him to death, and the Romans crucified him just this past Friday. We had our hopes up that he was the one about to deliver Israel."

"Hmmm," the stranger muttered.

Isaac jumped in, also excited. "Today is the third day since it happened, and this morning some of the women in our group completely confused us. Early this morning they went to his tomb, and they couldn't find his body. They came back to us with an incredible story. There were angels at the tomb who said he was alive. Can you believe it? We watched him die a bloody, painful death."

Cleopas cut Isaac off to finish the story. "So, some of our other friends immediately went back to the tomb to see if it was true. Was the body gone? Were angels there? They found the tomb empty, just as the women said, but they didn't see Jesus or the angels."

The stranger stopped and turned toward his walking companions. He studied their faces and smiled gently, but when he spoke, his words left them reeling. "My friends, you are very thick-headed and slow-hearted. Why can't you simply believe? Don't you see? Weren't you taught? These things had to happen. The Messiah had to suffer, to bleed as a living sacrifice for sin, to rise again into his glory at the right hand of the Father."

"Thick-headed and slow-hearted? Who is this man to say these things to us?" Cleopas wondered out loud. But then both men marveled at everything the stranger recounted about the Scriptures, starting at the beginning with the Book of Genesis and walking them through the story of Moses and all the prophets, and relating everything in the Word that pointed to the Messiah. Isaac's mind raced to contain it, and Cleopas was sure they had received the equivalent of a Yeshiva school education in one afternoon.

"Who is this man?" Cleopas whispered to his friend.

The last four miles passed quickly, and they reached Emmaus and the home of Cleopas' family. Something about this stranger drew them, and rather than part with Him, they urged Him to stay and share a meal. Here was a stranger with personal impact. Something about Him touched them, and they were not willing to see Him leave.

"Stay and have supper with us." Isaac and Cleopas both encouraged the stranger to stay. "It will be dark soon. The day is finished for walking. Please come in and join our family and friends."

When the stranger sat down with them in Cleopas' home, he was offered bread. He took the bread and gave thanks for it. Then he broke it and gave it to them. In those four actions their blindness became sight, their preoccupation became focus, their ignorance became knowledge and their doubt became true faith.

This was not the first time Cleopas and Isaac had witnessed this breaking of bread. In fact, they had been among the disciples to witness Jesus breaking bread when he was alive … and having his body broken.

On Friday's Roman cross, Jesus had performed the sacrifice that would redeem humanity—the offering of His body as the bread, the giving of thanks for God's love, the breaking of His body, and the shedding of His blood as sacrifice for the forgiveness of sins.

At that moment Cleopas, Isaac, and others at the table recognized the stranger's identity—here was Jesus, who really was their Messiah. Wide-eyed and humbled, they fully acknowledged and believed in Jesus as the true Messiah. They did not understand the entire scope of what this would mean, but a lifetime adventure and walk with the Redeemer awaited them.

They bowed down and worshipped Jesus as the Messiah, and then he disappeared. Without wasting a minute, Cleopas, Isaac, and their friends set out to return to Jerusalem and tell everyone they knew in the city what they had seen. Jesus was alive, walking, talking, eating.

When they found the eleven apostles of Jesus in Jerusalem, Cleopas told the story. "As He talked with us on the road and opened up the Scriptures to us, I felt a fire within. His words and wisdom, filled with the breath of God, kindled knowledge within me. We walked and talked with the resurrected Savior. It's really happened! Jesus has been raised from the dead. Jesus *is* the Messiah, the Son of God!"

In this Luke account of the Emmaus Road encounter, Cleopas and his companion Isaac, preoccupied with the events of the day and lost in their own fears and concerns, almost missed the One who would change their lives forever. Instead, their eyes and hearts were opened to the Son of God, and they began a great adventure—a lifelong Walk with the living Savior, from the Emmaus Road to wherever the journey might lead them.

OUR EMMAUS ROAD

Our "Emmaus Road" represents the life we walk before we meet Jesus in a personal and life-changing way. Sometimes our Emmaus Road can extend for decades—miles and miles of living. Some may never open their eyes to the reality and assurance of the One who walks beside them. But always He is there, walking beside us, waiting for us to turn our eyes to Him, anticipating we will recognize and acknowledge Him and the hope He offers.

Like Cleopas and Isaac, my day to recognize the living Savior and Lover of my soul would come unexpectedly. My Emmaus encounter began my walk on Layton, a new Walk, a new way.

The long road of following after the Savior in the daily Walk of life began right where I lived—on Layton. Eyes open to His presence, Jesus was there—in the lonely hours of the night, in the rejection, in the questions when I struggled to understand what it all meant—there was the One I had never noticed. There was Jesus. This change of focus and direction would forever affect and influence my Layton Walk, my struggle to follow Him, my attempts to stay on His road and live the way He showed me.

Layton living became a daily Walk with God, a journey with a purpose, a trek off the beaten cultural path, a hike of obedience to God's plan, an ordinary, daily life infused with God.

Did God's forgiveness change the damage done on my Emmaus Road of ignorance? It did not. Rejection, divorce, single parenting, financial struggles, loneliness were some of the battle scars.

The difference, post-Emmaus, hinged on learning to live as He wanted, recognizing my identity of wholeness in Christ, and seeking to face each moment as He willed, despite my anger and pain.

The Emmaus decision to recognize and accept Christ changed forever the direction and purpose of my life. It pointed me Godward.

I could no longer blame my former selfish life on the notion "I was just a quirky personality who made many mistakes." I was a full-fledged sinner, and the evidence of that saturated my life.

How do you get a do-over when you've made a mess of your character and choices? How do you erase the slate and start again? Only by immersing in the love and forgiveness of Jesus.

That's where the Walk with Jesus had to begin—on my knees with the realization and confession of who I am before a holy God. Before Him I have not one righteous, unsullied bone in my body. This is the identity Christ changed when I acknowledged His sacrifice as the only One who could make me acceptable before a holy God. He made me a new creation, pure and clean, standing firmly under the umbrella of His cleansing blood, washed by forgiveness, loved and accepted.

Jesus, the Gentle Gentleman, offers this clean slate to us and awaits our invitation. He waited nearly three decades for mine—enough time for my tongue and wrong attitudes to do a world of harm to myself and others. When He stepped into my life with mercy, He took my hand, became my best friend, and asked me to follow His Way and walk with Him. This is the trailhead for the remainder of our journeys. This is the beginning of our Walk.

Part 1
The Walk Begins

*"Thus says God, the LORD,
who created the heavens and stretched them out,
who spread out the earth and what comes from it,
who gives breath to the people on it
and spirit to those who walk in it:
I am the LORD; I have called you in righteousness;
I will take you by the hand and keep you…"*

Isaiah 42:5-6

1. Dead End

We had weekend guests from Connecticut when my husband Jack came home from work and went immediately to our bedroom. When he didn't return downstairs after a few minutes to join me and the other couple, I went upstairs to find him in our bedroom stuffing his suitcase with clothes.

"Business trip? What's going on?" I asked as he hurried to pack, his back toward me.

"I have to do this," he said without emotion, not turning around.

"Do what? What are you doing?" I could hear my voice rising.

"I'm leaving—now." Without glancing at me, Jack went to the closet and rummaged through some ties, grabbed a handful and haphazardly tossed them into the suitcase, slamming it shut.

Before I could grasp what was happening, he rushed past me out the bedroom door. I stood still and watched him stomp down the stairs and go out the front door, shutting it firmly behind him. Rousing myself, I hurried down the steps in pursuit, I stepped out on the porch in time to see him throw his suitcase over the driver's seat, climb behind the wheel of his black Corvette, and slam the door. I headed for the driver's side door, but the car had already headed down the driveway. The headlights came on, and I watched the sports car swerve around the corner on Layton, the red glow of the rear lights fading as completely as my hope.

He was gone. No explanations, no arguments.

Our Connecticut friends joined me in the driveway to greet Jack, only to find he had left without a word to them. Camaraderie with old friends impossible, I hurried upstairs. I needed to be with the boys. Two-year-old Bryan and two-month-old Trevor slept soundly after a busy day with our company, without a clue their father had stepped out of our family, perhaps out of our lives.

Only one year before, I had committed my life to Jesus. He was no longer a topic in Sunday School or an historical figure. He had become real, and I now had a relationship with the God who had forgiven me and prized me, who wanted to walk life with me, who gave me value. But the decision to follow Jesus, barely a year old, suddenly came face-to-face with the greatest pain I had ever known. How could this happen? I had no strength to tread the waters ahead. Why was God allowing this to happen to me if He loved me and wanted the best for me? I cried and I prayed out loud. "God, I know you don't want our marriage to fail! Lord, the children! They need a father. I can't do this. This isn't the way it's supposed to be."

In the months and years ahead, my emotions ran from despair to hopelessness to sorrow and rejection. I had trouble maneuvering my roller coaster of emotions, but the greater need was to parent my sons. My love tank was empty. How could I fill theirs? And this is when the miracle began to happen.

God, who has perfect timing and knows exactly the right thing to do, began to gently draw and hold me and my boys. Each day as I cried and emptied my heart before Him, He moved me bit by bit to dependence on Him—in the ruins of my life on Layton. God had known the path my life would take, and He had drawn me into relationship with Him—before life fell apart when the Corvette pulled out and turned the corner on Layton.

God preserved me in the ruins on my knees as I learned of His sufficiency. Through the years He has reminded me continually that He would never leave or forsake me. He would be an ever-present help in trouble. He would hear my prayers and speak gentle love and encouragement through His Word.

Marriage 'til death do us part was the promise I made, the commitment I intended to keep to my husband and to my children. I would be faithful, no matter what.

So, for sixteen years I held onto my marriage to Jack—despite the betrayals and abandonment, despite the fact that he did not even live in our home during those years. I prayed our family would be reunited, and we would be a whole family for God's glory. God does miracles. He could save our family and bring my husband home, no matter how impossible it appeared.

It did not happen, and after sixteen years of separation and a child by another woman, I released my hope to a divorce court. Those years encompassed the growing-up years of my sons Bryan and Trevor, who were ages eighteen and sixteen when the divorce process started. The voyage rocked us daily, but God's care never failed. He brought us through the storm, battered and beaten but stronger. His plans were not my plans.

Now, I rest on the other side of the locust swarm of rejection, abandonment, single parenting. Here, there are still waters, green pastures, and joy, including two daughters-in-law, Janine and Casie, and six wonderful grandchildren. Harried relationships, wasted time, missed opportunities, frustration, anger—these lost years have been redeemed. God has blessed us.

Have you felt the dark clouds of oppression and despair follow you for too long? Trouble, pain, heartache—these are opportunities to lean into Christ, to place your cares in His hands where your name is engraved.

Sometimes a beginning has to start with an end. We have to go through the valley to get to the top of the mountain.

Our ever-faithful God hears our cries for help. He may not answer the way we think He should, but in His wisdom, He answers in the way that is best for our good and His glory. Lean on His love and sufficiency to carry you through every valley. Turn to Him when the landscape is bleak, and the crop is ruined. In due time, the darkness will lift, and He will repay you for the lost crops the locusts have eaten with fullness, wonders, and joy.

Encouragement for Your Walk

"But one thing I do: Forgetting what is behind and straining toward what is ahead, I press on toward the goal to win the prize for which God has called me heavenward in Christ Jesus" (Philippians 3:13-14).

The Walk requires perseverance when the road is a mine field of trouble and disappointments. It requires endurance for the long-haul. Always the Walk involves drawing close daily to the One who knows us best and loves us with an everlasting love. He will not reject us when we commit to following His Way. As we walk with Him each day, He will give us the power to endure and persevere. Eyes off the past, looking Godward. His plan and purpose will surface. Press on faithfully down your road. Press on.

Lord, help us to walk with perseverance, focusing on Jesus and on your faithful love. Help us to forgive those who have hurt us, to put offenses in the past, and to lean into You.

2. The Trailhead

My Emmaus Road Encounter, the day I finally gave my full attention to Jesus and believed His sacrifice for me, actually took place in Wolcott, Connecticut, just one year before my husband climbed in the Corvette and left home. To outward appearances, my life looked good. But—there were questions, the main one being, "I've got everything a girl could want so why am I thinking, '*Is this all there is?*'" Holes riddled paradise. What was I missing?

A teaching career in a local school district right out of college, a new home and car, a handsome husband, and a beautiful new baby—weren't these all of the things a girl growing up in the 1960s wanted? If I had everything a girl could want, why did I feel it wasn't enough or something important just wasn't there? Of course, our paradise had a few snags: Why was my husband working late so often? Why did a cold wall go up every time I drew near him? "Where were you last night?" I cried. "Let's talk about our problems," I pleaded. The absence of sensitivity on both sides generally added a few more stones to a growing wall.

If Jesus had been walking with me, if He awaited my attention, even if He reached for my hand, I walked insensible to His gentle call, engrossed in my needy self-centered life.

"Where were you last night?" I interrogated Jack after one particular 2 a.m. return home.

"I worked until 10 p.m. then a few of us went out after work,"

"Couldn't you have called?" I asked.

"I didn't think of it. We were busy."

"Who were you with?"

"Just some of the guys."

When it happened again a few nights later, I tried calling Jack's office phone several times. He never answered. *Will he say he was working again tonight?* I wondered.

The deception continued. My anxiety grew. It seemed impossible infidelity might have its foot in our door. This was the man who pledged love, family ... the world. We had been sweethearts since high school and faithful friends through a six-month separation while I was in school in England. How many letters crossed the Atlantic pledging forever love and looking toward a future and family together. *What happened?*

I needed a supportive husband. I needed his attention. I wanted his love. I needed... I wanted ... I, I, I. What is there to give when all love is focused inward? What I really needed was for my eyes to be focused on the One who is perfect love and to learn His ways of selflessness, mercy, and kindness in my relationship with my husband—to be able to give to him what I wanted for myself. He had the same emotional needs as me, but we both fell deeper into our narrowly focused wants, and apart from one another.

As with Cleopas on the Emmaus Road, Jesus never forced Himself into my company, but there came a day when my eyes opened to the Stranger's presence. A neighbor invited me to her church. At first, I sloughed off the invite, thinking it an unnecessary addition to my schedule since my church attendance ended in college.

But while on maternity leave from teaching with baby Bryan and without a stringent schedule, I accepted my neighbor Claire's invitation to attend a Bible study across the street in her home. Perhaps the camaraderie of other women drew me, even though I acted as a devil's advocate almost every evening as they studied Scripture. "How do you know this to be true?" I'd ask. "Seems impossible! I don't see God in my life." I questioned their conversations and assumptions. Nevertheless, I returned each week.

Eventually, two women from the church came to my home. As I invited Pat and Sue to sit at my kitchen table, Sue volunteered to play with Bryan. *That's kind,* I thought, *otherwise we won't have much conversation.* I had attended my neighbor's church, and I assumed these ladies were a women's team to welcome visitors to their church.

Pat opened our conversation with a challenge. "If you were to die today, do you know whether you would go to heaven?" *Heaven? What a way to start a conversation with someone you don't know!*

But, strangely, a topic like heaven suddenly sounded good. Had I ever really thought of heaven since I was a child at Mt. Bethel Church back home on Layton? Now, pregnant, mothering a toddler, out of the professional milieu, and trying to understand my husband's coolness and our disconnect, I responded that I certainly hoped I would go to heaven.

But was disobedience to my parents as a teen a disqualifier? Were those times my boyfriend, now husband, and I did questionable things going to keep me out? Was our unhappy paradise an elimination factor?

Pat opened her Bible and read a string of verses.

- *"For all have sinned and fall short of the glory of God"* (Romans 3:23). No question about that.
- *"For the wages of sin is death, but the gift of God is eternal life in Christ Jesus our Lord"* (Romans 6:23).
- *"If you declare with your mouth 'Jesus is Lord,' and believe in your heart that God raised Him from the dead, you will be saved"* (Romans 10:9).

Too much. I couldn't keep up. I needed to process this. Surely, I had heard all of this in the past. Why did it suddenly now seem new and very important? "Would you like to ask Jesus to forgive your sins and come into your life?" Pat asked me.

Of course I would.

"If you accept Jesus' forgiveness, you are His child," she said. It made sense. I had been raised in the church, attended a Christian college—but never had my heart been so in need of love and so open to this invitation. When Pat asked me to pray with her, it was the logical next step.

"Yes, Jesus, I want to be forgiven," I said out loud. "I want to be yours. I want to learn to live your way."

Pat had clearly presented God's saving grace and my need of it. As surely as with Cleopas and his companions, my eyes opened to the living

Savior—and I knew who He was—and I would come to realize who I was in Him. Self-centeredness, pride, meanness, ignorance. The One whose body had been broken, given, and offered had forgiven these sins, my sins, and more.

There was no way to explain this 180-degree turn in my life, except as an act of a God who loved me, distant and disconnected as I was. He knew my future and the trouble ahead. In His love He wanted to draw me into His arms, into the safety and security of a relationship with Him, a relationship which saved my life in the years ahead when desperation came knocking.

When my husband came home from work the evening Pat and Sue visited, I couldn't wait to tell him what I had learned and the step I had taken to commit myself to Jesus.

"I finally get it!" I gushed. "God loves us and has a plan for our lives. Being a Christian is about having a relationship with a living God who loves us."

By the look on my husband's face, I could tell I'd said too much too fast. Perhaps Jack was not ready for this God-talk, this conviction.

But I knew this Emmaus Road Encounter at the age of twenty-eight transformed my reality. A sinner, unfit to stand in the presence of a Holy God but loved beyond measure by her Father Creator, came face-to-face with forgiveness, acceptance, mercy, and grace. Suddenly, I knew all of my previous life events were part of the divine plan, part of the map that led and prepared me for this revelation, this choice, on my Emmaus Road.

Encouragement for Your Walk

Have you wondered if you would go to heaven if you were to die today? No reason to wonder. Scripture is clear: *"Believe in the Lord Jesus Christ and you will be saved"* (Acts 16:31). Saved for an eternity in heaven, saved for a relationship with your Creator God here on earth. A black and white decision—accept or reject His offer. Set your life on a new course. Thank Him for the sacrifice He made for your sins that day long ago on

Calvary. The Son of God, the only acceptable sacrifice, has laid down His life for your redemption. Open your eyes and see who walks beside you daily on your Emmaus Road.

    God, I want to know you. I want to know the endless scope and significance of life beyond my narrow vision. I want to understand and walk with the One who loves me unconditionally. Open my eyes to You.

3. Walking Alone

The bed creaked with each movement. I burrowed further under the quilt, seeking a deeper refuge. My pillow jabbed with pin pricks of feathers and stirred me, but I buried my face in it and sobbed.

Downstairs, I heard my baby's cry and my mother's voice murmuring lovingly to him. Two-month-old Trevor with his chocolate eyes and ready smile was pleasant, pliable, happy, any mother's delight. But I lay submerged in the sea of my bed and my fears. "Bye-o-my baby," I heard Mom singing her old lullaby to Trevor. I envisioned him cuddled in her arms as she rocked.

Weeping and vocalizing my pain into the folds of my covers, I opened my eyes to Mom now standing beside my bed. No accusations. No recriminations. Wordlessly, she opened the bedroom window and left the room, allowing me time to grieve. The August sun beamed and the sounds of late summer intruded into my dark world. What I heard of summer sent me sobbing, yet again, into an already damp pillow.

Two-year-old Bryan romped around the yard with our beagle puppy Snoopy, who barked his wild hound sound and sent Bryan into fits of laughter. His feet pitter-pattered under my window—Snoopy in hot pursuit. "MaMa," he called to my mother. "Come play with me!" And my mother joined him, singing, "Ring around the Rosie ... we all fall down."

Falling down. Depression had held me in bed for over a week. Mom, who lived next door, had taken time off from work to care for the two boys and me. She carried my load each day, trying to provide a lifeline. *If I could just fade into oblivion*, I grieved. *Mom would be a better parent to my boys than I could ever be. She has proven herself. I've failed as a wife, and now as a mother.*

Recently, when my husband Jack came home from work, he packed his suitcase and my self-esteem and left. The grass smelled sweeter, the sun shone brighter for him—somewhere else. *What happened to 'until death us do part'? What happened to 'You're the most wonderful girl in the world? I'll always love you.'?* Promises broken. I only knew that my mountain had fallen into the sea with my dreams of family and future, and I was drowning in its surging waters.

Now, Mom sat beside me on the bed.

"OK, Jo. Enough. You need to get up and care for your children."

Was she kidding? The task was beyond me. Mom had always spoken and lived with wisdom and authority. I trusted her. She had a tough strain of "can do" in every situation. If she said that I needed to get up and care for the children, she meant for it to happen. But how? Fear, anger, and pain had me in a stranglehold. I had nothing to give, and children needed parents.

I rolled over yet again and hid my face from her, angry with God for allowing this disaster to happen to our family. It seemed my life had reached an irreversible dead end.

A year before, I had been introduced to Jesus' saving grace and the gift of relationship with Him. But in the months since then with the birth of the baby, my husband's job change, and his aversion to my new church attendance, my friendship with Jesus stalled. Here in this bed, God had my attention. *If you are really there, Jesus, if you really care about us, please, Lord, help!*

"Get up. Go to your children." Not my mother's voice this time, Jesus called. Step-by-baby-step over the course of weeks … months. "Get up. Go to your children. Live." I moved back into life, tiny bits at a time, for the emotional and spiritual load I carried seemed exceedingly heavy.

Because we had moved from Connecticut to Pennsylvania in the past year, my friend connections were weak, but within months of the move and before Trevor's birth, neighbors had invited me to a Bible study.

God had gone ahead of me in this move between states and from wife to single mom. He had prepared a group of friends who would see me through the worst months ahead.

In that year between coming to Christ and returning to Pennsylvania, my grandmother died, leaving her house, right next door to my parents, available. God knew the events which would transpire in my life, and He prepared a friend group to soothe my pain in His Word and a home near my parents where I would have the support of my family. That was divine coverage.

When I searched for a teaching job and a way to support our family, everyone said, "You'll never get a job. They are too hard to come by, and when a job opens up, it goes to a relative of someone on the school board. Who do you know on the school board?"

God gave me a substitute teaching job which I worked for almost five years when the superintendent came to me with this suggestion: "I will move some faculty around to open up an English position. Then the job will be yours." I never filled out an application for the job or had an interview. A kind superintendent and God handed me the job I needed. But I also needed a babysitter for pre-school-aged Trevor if I was to teach full-time. Mom and Dad worked and could not help. Howard, an elderly neighbor who had never had children, went out on a shaky limb and volunteered. Help from an unexpected source, a kind neighbor, and God.

In time and over the years, Jesus continued to show me His presence, taught me of His provision, and gave me enough courage to raise my sons. My dependence had to be on God, not on my mother or on my husband. The daily song of my heart still rings true: "I need you, Lord."

I began to know personally the true Lover of my soul through His Word. One day in Bible study, I read Psalm 46:1-3: *"God is my refuge and strength, an ever-present help in trouble. Therefore, we will not fear, though the earth give way and the mountains fall into the heart of the sea, though its waters roar and foam and the mountains quake with their surging."* It became my song, stamped on my heart, uttered frequently and lavishly each day. The mountains had fallen in, the waters had washed over me, and God became my sufficient and dependable anchor. His ongoing whisper to my heart, "I will never leave or forsake you," echoed through my days.

Several years later, my parents retired and moved seven hundred miles away. Again, there was a wrenching sense of loss. Although I was taking shaky steps of dependence on God, I knew I had backup with my parents next door if my faith—and God—left me wanting.

Still, rejection and loss never moved far from the surface of my psyche. With my parents' move, any shred of opportunity to depend on someone else daily was eliminated. The mountains quaked again, and God called, "I am here. I will never leave or forsake you. My promise is written in Jesus' blood. You are my child, and I am faithful." God called through my Bible study with the girls. He called in the silence of the house when the boys were tucked in. He called when at 2 a.m. I cried yet again into my pillow. Bit by grueling bit, lonely day followed by desperate night, He drew me and drew me, and the years passed, and somehow, I was not consumed by or swallowed in the sea of remorse.

Incredibly, those two precious little boys and I stood, not alone, but safe in the hands of our Refuge and Strength. With Jesus you are never a single mom.

In retrospect, I praise God for giving me a wise mother. She insisted I get out of bed that first week of depression and live up to the responsibility I had been given. Her release of us to God gave me the great opportunity to be the mother God intended me to be, to raise my children, and to do it in dependence on Him. Trouble and hardship masquerade as pain, but their real name is Opportunity—the most significant opportunities of our lives are to live in dependence on God in all of life's turmoil.

Facing the challenges of single mothering or any of life's problems that storm us through the years, this sweet promise encouraged my heart, *"God is our refuge and strength, an ever-present help in trouble"* (Psalm 46:1).

Encouragement for Your Walk

Sometimes the Walk is an Everest climb. Mountains loom, floods wash us away, bottomless drop-offs frighten our stability, the balancing act of standing on a ledge overwhelms. Keeping in step with God on such a climb leaves us weak and wanting more of our Savior.

Nationally known author and pastor Alistair Begg wrote, "I can walk through the peaks and valleys of life with the assurance that I am loved by the one who made all things and directs all things, and because I never had to win His love, I can never lose it." God's love follows us and leads us. We are His.

Jehovah Jireh, our Provider, we need you to help us walk dangerous and disheartening roads. We need your strength. We need you to be our refuge. We may think we need many other things the world has to offer, but you are the answer to our deepest needs. Help us to know and experience your sufficiency during the most difficult journeys of our lives. Lord, we need you.

4. Cross-Bearing

Crosses. Too heavy. Too awkward. Overburdening our walk and affecting our spiritual movement, our emotional stability, perhaps even our physical stamina, our crosses make our walk arduous.

Bitterness and anger are among the crosses I've carried, the crosses I've had to learn how to put down. Putting down a cross is often harder than picking it up. Bitterness and anger have a sticking quality—they can be put down, but without careful and vigilant monitoring, they creep back into our hearts.

Walking life's road becomes difficult if we carry such loads, and most of us do. What's the burden you carry? Mine was being unable to forgive God, my husband Jack, or myself all those years when I remained married and miserable, feeling betrayed, unloved, abandoned and alone.

My cross finally became unbearable until I began my Walk on Emmaus, and Jesus helped me carry my cross, even when Jack left us and it became so heavy. Eventually, through forgiveness and healing, I could cast my cross aside and walk Layton Road with Jesus, happy and free.

Know this about your oppressive burdens—God is aware and He hears you. When your Layton Road or Maple Street or Main Avenue become an Everest trail, He sees. "Does he not see my ways and count my every step?" (Job 31:4) "His eyes are on the ways of mortals. He sees their every step" (Job 34:21). And He longs for us to walk the path of the redeemed, unfettered by the burdens, and able to lift our feet joyfully to look at the world around us with His eyes, not the clouded vision of a cross-bearer.

Jesus walked a difficult road called the Calvary Road. It took him to a hill where God asked Him to lay down His life in blood-drenched sacrifice for people who did not know Him or care. It was an act of obedience and love. The only sinless sacrifice, the only perfect and holy One fit to be offered for mankind. At the end of His road on Calvary, He willingly allowed soldiers to nail Him to a cross, and with His blood He unloaded the cross of sin He bore for us. Forgiveness was the gift He gave us on the cross He bore. With His death, He provided the way for all of us to also put down our crosses of sin at His feet and be forgiven.

Forgiveness is where putting down our crosses begins—asking God to forgive us. It's a choice. I had to eventually choose to turn my burden over to Him by saying, "I'm sorry. Please forgive me for the anger and bitterness I carry against Jack. Help me to forgive him. Take this load, Jesus." Then I kept casting my burden on Him every time it returned—and that was every day for a long time—laying it down, being forgiven, walking on, determined to step the way the Savior desired.

My bitterness and anger tagged me consistently, so asking for God's forgiveness and seeking to walk as He desired became a daily topic of my quiet time with Him ... until, years down the road, my heart and mind were awash in the joy of His presence and His love for me. Finally, I left my crosses beside the trail. Living with Him became the dominant tone, not focusing on how I had been hurt, how I had lost dramatically what others seemed to hold lightly, how offended I felt.

Horror turned to joy in Jesus' resurrection on the third day. It became the holiday we call Easter, although today's cultural celebrations have nothing to do with cross-bearing. Easter on Layton has annual familial traditions and plenty of fun, but the vision of a cross laid down has become a daily reminder, rather than a once-a-year holiday.

Easter family traditions for us included rising early on Easter morning for a sunrise service at Mt. Bethel Church or at Lackawanna State Park or at the end of Cherry Grove beach in South Carolina. Easter traditions always included church-going, new clothes, ham dinners,

Easter baskets hidden around the yard, egg hunts, traveling to Myrtle Beach for spring family reunions.

We followed these traditions as children; I practiced them with my children and now with my grandchildren. Carrying crosses seems to have little to do the holiday we celebrate today.

One significant change has occurred—my increasing realization that Easter should be celebrated every day of the year because Easter brings a precious hope of resurrection and eternal life and the soul-breaking relief of putting down our crosses and being forgiven.

Left to my own devices, I wouldn't have had a chance to meet God's standard of holiness nor would I have a chance to enter eternity in heaven with Him. Like you, I'm a sinner by birth—in need of Jesus' grace and mercy offered on His cross. Grateful for His cross laid down for us, and for the Emmaus Road encounter that helped me to recognize and acknowledge what He had done, I can walk now with assurance of His presence each day on the road and on into eternity.

Death and life—He has covered it all.

Now, His Spirit walks daily with those who have come to Him in repentance, giving help, comfort, encouragement, wisdom, guidance. We have been offered the opportunity to intimately know and experience Him—day-in and day-out, when the Walk is easy or when it causes us to flag and fail.

Jesus' cross and resurrection are not exclusive to residents of a country road in rural America. They stand as offers to people on Lombard Street in San Francisco, Abbey Road in London, the Hollywood Walk of Fame, the Las Vegas Strip, Wall Street, the *Champs Elysees*, or Orchard Road in Singapore—any street, any time in history.

Encouragement for Your Walk

"Get rid of bitterness, rage, and anger, brawling and slander, along with every form of malice. Be kind and compassionate to one another, forgiving each other, just as in Christ, God forgave you. Follow God's example, therefore, as dearly loved children, and walk in the way of love, just as Christ loved us and gave himself up for us as a

fragrant offering and sacrifice to God" (Ephesians 4:31-5:2).

Putting down the burden of our sins and accepting the forgiveness Christ offered on the cross will initiate spiritual freedom. Watch daily, slowly, as changes begin to happen in a life desiring to keep in step with Him, living as He desires. Remembering and celebrating Christ's redemption and forgiveness on the Cross and asking for forgiveness always should characterize our Walk every day, not just on Easter. Easter is an everyday holiday, meant to lighten your sin burden. Put down the crosses you carry at Jesus' feet. You will walk with a lighter step, perhaps even skipping, down your road today.

Lord, thank you for the sacrifice Jesus provided for us on the cross. Let our lives radiate the gratefulness and freedom of a soul redeemed and bound for heaven at the end of our road. Help us to daily lay our crosses, our sins, at your feet. Implant the joy of forgiveness across our demeanors and groom your love in us.

5. The Trail Guide

Yes, my walk on Layton began with my first Bible study.

The Bible, I discovered, was a map, a divine plan for how to live each day. No question, I needed directions to navigate the pocked and potholed road I traveled. Life's twists proved my instincts were often wrong. I needed a compass to point me to true North every day.

Throughout the years Bible studies became a focal point of my life. I've discovered studying God's Word motivates, convicts, directs, comforts, challenges, and inspires. Bible study shows us how to live in God's Way on life's journey. In God's Word I have come to know this One who loves me gracefully, mercifully, and completely, this One who promises never to leave or forsake me, this One who forgives and saves a sinner like me.

But there was one Bible study along the way that really made a difference in my Walk.

One summer I joined ladies in our church again to read God's Word through a lovely study called *Wonderstruck: Awaken to the Nearness of God* by Margaret Feinberg.

Margaret defined "wonder" as being awed by the presence and action of God in our daily lives. She encouraged us to live "eyes wide open" to see God's handiwork, His blessings, and His presence. Each day we watched expectantly for God and recorded three wonders in our journals. "Wonders" like the scent of a newborn child, a fading sunset, a word of kindness, the crunch of an almond, or much-needed rain. We were never disappointed.

We found God everywhere, all the time. The friend who called when

I felt particularly lonely. A bouquet of flowers delivered to school on my first day. A group of college kids showing up in my kitchen with a few boxes of pasta to cook dinner for a single mom and her two little boys. Grandma's pot of soup waiting in the backseat when I left a busy day at school. A package of autumn napkins left anonymously at my back door and tied with pretty ribbon. A neighbor carrying up my garbage can. A friend plowing six inches of snow from my driveway. Dad replacing tiles in the bathroom ceiling. Bryan climbing a ladder to put leaf guards on all the rain gutters. Trevor and Casie preparing a gravel pad and the yard for a garage. When I paid attention, I realized God sent acts of love every day to say, "I see you, I know you, I love you." God's presence was tangible through other people.

My experiences confirmed Psalm 40:5. *"Many, LORD my God, are the wonders you have done, the things you planned for us. None can compare with you; were I to speak and tell of your deeds, they would be too many to declare."*

We tend to live at breakneck speed, missing the hand of God as surely as a car hurling down the highway at seventy-five miles per hour misses the delicate beauty of a daisy beside the road. Apply the brakes, open our eyes, wait expectantly, and be surprised by His wonder. These lessons resound in our hearts as we seek to develop the discipline of seeing God.

There He is in the yellows, purples, pinks of spring flowers. There He is in the unexpected phone call from an old friend. There He is in the lavish gift of supplies for a mission trip. Or a mother-in-law's supply of school polo shirts for the boys. We have savored His sweet presence with us, we have recognized His divine handiwork, and we are awed. *"Who among the gods is like you, LORD? Who is like you—majestic in holiness, awesome in glory, working wonders?" (Psalm 17:7)*.

This readiness for discovery whets our appetites for a vibrant intimacy with God. We awake, curious to know Him more. A. W. Tozer's sentiments become our own. "I want the presence of God Himself, or I don't want anything at all to do with religion. I want all that God has or I don't want any."

Live "eyes wide open."

Lord, you leave me Wonderstruck on Layton.

JO ANN WALCZAK

Encouragement for Your Walk

"Keep your eyes open for God, watch for His works; be alert for signs of His presence. Remember the world of wonders He has made, His miracles ..." (Psalm 105:4-5 *The Message*). Living with our eyes and ears alert, searching, open to God's presence on our Walk is the challenge. When we look around with awareness of His proximity, we will spy God and the actions He inspires on our behalf. Seeing love hugs from God will enrich our days and satisfy our heart's need for closeness and care.

Lord, give us eyes-wide open to see You at work around us. When we look down and turn inward on our daily Walk, Lord, we fail to see the huge array of love and beauty you offer. Bits of joy surround us if we aren't watching our feet. Please keep our heads up, eyes roaming to the wonders you offer us every day of the journey.

Part 2
Bumps in the Road

*"'I will lead the blind by ways they have not known,
along unfamiliar paths I will guide them;
I will turn the darkness into light before them
and make the rough places smooth.
These are the things I will do;
I will not forsake them'."*

Isaiah 42:16

6. Thieves!

Gone! My wedding ring, my grandmother's gold bracelet, a few necklaces—gone. I searched my dresser and jewelry boxes again. I knew instantly my valuables were not in the usual storage spaces. Had I moved them? Was I overlooking them tucked in a hidden corner? No. The only valuable jewelry I owned was gone.

Every Sunday morning found me in church, but on the Sunday of the robbery, I knew something screamed trouble when I reached the back door. A crack the width of the wooden door showed that force had been applied. A knife had carved out the area around the latch. Oblivious to danger within, I entered and toured the downstairs, then the upstairs. It didn't appear that anything had been taken—not the television, the computer, or any items I thought an enterprising thief might grab. The house looked just as I had left it.

But when I went to change my Sunday clothes and put away my jewelry, I knew instantly the dresser had been rearranged. I looked through my jewelry box and random containers to discover several items missing, at least those of any value in a mess of gawdy costume stuff. Nana had given me her gold bangle when I was a teen. My gold wedding band measured about a half-inch wide. Engraved on the inside with my husband's name and mine, it too was special and nostalgic. Someone knew what to look for. Someone knew I would not be home on Sunday morning.

Victimized again? My heart had been smashed. My valuables stolen. The "poor me" chorus ramped up again.

I called the police. An officer in blue, draped in artillery and badge ID, knocked on my door shortly after. Instantly, I knew I had good help—it was Frank. I hadn't seen him for twenty years since he livened up my seventh grade English classes. Now, he had a position on our police force. My anxiety level dipped. I knew Frank could be trusted. I'd seen him hold his own in junior high school. I knew his dependability. He would help. Frank swept the dresser for fingerprints and searched the house, closets, basements, cubby holes, even the coal bin in the far corner of the basement. I followed him like a puppy until all hidey-holes were investigated and my house declared safe.

A stranger with evil intent had roamed through my home like a prowling lion, seeking to steal what did not belong to him or her.

Discovering a thief had been in my home reminded me of my suspicion that an Enemy also roamed the halls of my heart. The Enemy had tantalized my mind on numerous occasions with, "Who do you think you are? You are a divorced, single parent. You have nothing to offer other people. You wouldn't be a divorced, single parent if you had something to offer a husband or the world." The Enemy knew all the buttons to push to rip up my self-esteem and plunge me into depression. He is a master of lies. "Once a victim, always a victim," he whispered. The Enemy stole my peace by causing me to wonder, *Was I making wrong choices? Had disobedience hampered my relationship with God? Why did I feel sometimes so distant and disconnected from God? Was I even safe anymore in my home? Why me?*

Doubts and discouragement like these are the stock in trade of the Enemy. He revels in causing us to question God's faithfulness. He laughs when I wonder why God loves me. He rejoices when my spirit is weighted with regrets and guilt. He delights in stealing my peace. He made me his victim long before anyone broke into my home.

As surely as a thief invaded my home and stole my jewelry, the Enemy committed a home invasion in my heart, stealing my confidence, joy, and intimacy with Christ. I was a victim of the Enemy—too often.

The police offered a few helpful suggestions: always lock doors, purchase a security system, and install motion detector lighting around the exterior of my home.

God's Word also warns us to anticipate the Enemy's attack. "Be strong in the Lord and strength of His might," God tells us. "*Be alert and of sober mind. Your enemy the devil prowls around like a roaring lion looking for someone to devour*" (1 Peter 5:8). Expect him to play havoc with your mind and heart. Don't be surprised when it happens and hold on to God's truth: you are loved with an everlasting love.

We are called to take the offensive, to be watchful, to run from sin and evil, to obey God's commands, to rest in His care and sovereignty. The Enemy works to derail our Walk with Jesus and our focus on Him, but in Jesus the victory is won. Our hearts are secured for Him.

When you sense thieves at the door of your heart house, and discouragement and despair attempt to rob the joy of relationship with Christ, run to Jesus for strength and protection.

Thieves come to steal, but Jesus came to give—a life more precious than gold.

Encouragement for Your Walk

"*The thief comes only to steal and kill and destroy,*" Jesus said, but "*I have come that they may have life, and have it to the full*" (John 10:10). The Evil One, the Thief, walks daily on our journey with us. He is eager to discourage us and cause us to doubt God and His promises.

He plants stumbling holes and hurdles along our Walk to distract our focus from Jesus. Has he stolen your self-esteem? Has he convinced you of your unworthiness to be loved? Has he made you think you are a failure? When the thief comes to steal your joy and assurance, run, don't walk—to Jesus. Dwell on His promises of presence and help. Memorize some Bible verses to keep your mind and heart standing firmly with Jesus.

Lord, keep us watchful for evil and the enemy's distractions as we walk. Heighten our sensitivity to the Evil One's wiles and siren song. Strengthen our devotion to you and our faithfulness to walking the road that honors you. Help us to realize that in Christ we are not victims—we are victors.

7. What's in a Name?

The name "Jo Ann" never caught on in American culture really. As a schoolteacher for many years, I had thousands of students, including an abundance of Jennifers, Emilys, Ashleys, Megans, Sarahs, Amys, Amandas, but I can't remember even <u>one</u> Jo Ann. The name lacks the star quality and pertness of a "Jennifer" Anniston or "Sarah" Jessica Parker. Cultural "name" trends, spurred by Hollywood, produced only "Joanne" Woodward, and the "name" stopped there.

Through the years the name "Jo Ann" has been a source of continual frustration when it comes to spelling. "Joanne, Jo Anne, Joann" are a few of the variety of ways the name can be spelled. Employed for twenty-seven years in the same school district, my employer spelled my name incorrectly on my retirement certificate. A close family relative has yet to get my name right on gifts and birthday cards, and even Social Security has produced a dictionary worth of trouble with the misspelling.

Imagine my surprise last month when I opened an email with a photo of a Chinese girl holding a sign with my name—spelled correctly. This child lives in an orphanage in western China. A friend of mine worked at the orphanage for six weeks one summer among a minority group called the Yi people. Because Chinese names prove challenging for the Westerner, my friend gave the children English names. She named this little Yi girl—Jo Ann. No cultural pressure for trendy names there. And small chance that I will forget to pray for my namesake on the other side of the world.

Still, I guess our family has done well by the name. I have had the unique privilege of bearing the names of both my mother and father. Joseph married Annette, and the union produced their first of three daughters who was named "Jo Ann," a little of mom, a little of dad. Bryan and Janine did a wonderful thing when their first daughter was born. They gave her the name Anna, after Grandma Jo Ann and Great-grandma Annette. Anna is a much lovelier form of the name. And Trev and Casie honored family tradition when their first daughter was born: Kassadee Ann because, as Trev said, "I'm sure you will be very involved with her."

Names carry weight and significance. Even road names can be identifiers. Layton refers to an early settler in Justus. Emmaus means "hot springs" in Greek, marking it as a place someone might enjoy visiting. Layton will forever have positive connotations for me. We would like our personal names to have the same positive connotation in the minds of others.

"What's in a name?" Juliet bemoaned to her lover, Romeo, in Shakespeare's classic play, *Romeo and Juliet*.

Romeo's family name, "Montague," caused much chagrin for Juliet's parents because it represented an unacceptable union for her with a despised family. Juliet tells Romeo,

"O, be some other name!

What's in a name? That which we call a rose

By any other name would smell as sweet." (Act II, Scene II, *Romeo and Juliet*)

What Juliet meant is, it only matters what something or someone is, not what they are called.

True, Juliet, but "name" still carries a boatload of importance. Names are identified with our characters or our families. In Jesus' day, a name reflected identity, sometimes aspects of God's character, or life events. The name "Jesus means Yahweh saves."

Some boys are named after their fathers, and they bear the tag "Junior" or "III or IV." I even know a family whose son is called "Bob Five," fifth of the Bob line. Girls are sometimes given their mother's name.

Yes, a name bears connection and identity.

Nowhere is that connection and identity of name more significant than in God's Kingdom. In Isaiah 43:16 God says, *"I have summoned you by name: you are mine."* God knows our names. More than that, He knows the essence of who we are. He knows us.

Isaiah 49:15-18 says, *"Can a mother forget the infant at her breast, walk away from the baby she bore? But even if mothers forget, I'd never forget you—never. Look, I've written your names on the palms of my hands."* Imagine that. Jesus' blood has tattooed our names for eternity on His hands. Simply wonderful.

Those who acknowledge the sacrifice that God made of His Son Jesus for our sins are eternally remembered in the "Book of Life." Revelation 21:27 reminds us that only those whose names are written in the Lamb's Book of Life will be in heaven.

Revelation 3:5 says, *"I will never blot out the name of that person from the book of life but will acknowledge that name before my Father and His angels."*

What's in a name? The sweet grace of our Father's love—no misspellings, no mistakes.

Your name and identity, whether a Yi orphan in the remote parts of western China or a retired grandmother in suburban America, are preserved forever with God.

Encouragement for Your Walk

When on our Walk, we feel forgotten, inconsequential, unimportant, remember this: God knows your name. He knows you. He holds your hand and your life. *"See, I have written your name on the palms of my hand"* (Isaiah 49:16).

Lord, keep us always in mind of our value to you because of the sacrifice of Jesus. You know each of our missteps, every word misspoken, each rash act, every desire of our hearts, and you continue to love us—anyway. Thank you for knowing our names.

8. Roots to Breathe

Some of my vital roots were lost one January. I watched my beloved ninety-eight-year-old father step into eternity, which was followed a few days later by my milestone birthday, one that our society uses as a gateway to old age. Dad's death produced deep grief. And my birthday reminded me of years squandered, people gone, time passing. Loss. The Walk slowed again.

I had to remind myself to stop and breathe.

Sometimes, breathing requires thought, intention. Sometimes, we need to find reasons for its natural ebb and flow or catch it when there's a pause like a stomach punch or a slap to the emotions.

That January had some breathless moments, moments that required reflection, regrouping, reconsidering. Time to breathe. God knows our gasp, the skipped heartbeat, the need to intentionally inhale life when the wind has been knocked out of us.

"Breathe" has become a popular cultural admonition, bandied about often when someone is overexcited, stressed, or depressed. I've heard friends advise each other to "breathe." Not because they've stopped breathing, but because life caught them off guard. One local yoga salon even calls itself "Breathe." The idea behind the word? Slow down. Contemplate.

That winter, I went to Florida, a haven for America's elderly who may be contemplating their next breath. I needed to breathe—deeply. To "breathe," my old friends and I walked, each day, through one of the lovely parks in the Sarasota-Tampa Bay area: the Robinson Preserve, Coquina Beach on Anna Maria Island, Emerson Point Park, Selby

Botanical Gardens, Myakka State Park, and Ringling's *Ca' d'Zan* mansion.

The Creator draws powerful lessons for us from His Creation. Walks in these Florida parks left me with one overwhelming impression: Roots Rule. It is the incomparable power of roots that enables survival in the face of destruction. Roots, God reminded me, enable breathing.

Mangroves and banyans dot and edge these parks. The secret to their endurance and survival in a harsh environment is their roots, roots the Creator has groomed to breathe in the most difficult circumstances.

Mangroves, a twisted jumble of trees and shrubs growing along rivers and shores in the tropics, are distinctive because they flourish from a tangle of roots. One mangrove seedling sends many roots into the soil eventually spreading into an entire thicket, becoming a birthplace and home for all kinds of creatures. The mangroves spawn a rich ecosystem along the coast.

Mangroves grow remarkably tough, primarily because of their incredible capacity to put down roots that provide oxygen for respiration. Some mangroves produce pencil-like roots that stick out of the mud like snorkels. The roots are covered with breathing pores that can close to keep them from drowning.

Despite the twice-a-day flooding by tides that would kill any other tree, despite the salty water that is one hundred times saltier than what other plants can tolerate, despite ocean storms and hurricanes, the mangrove thrives and multiplies, remaining remarkably resilient and strong in the buffeting, battering circumstances of its environment because of its unique breathing roots.

Banyan trees reconfirm the power of roots. The world's biggest trees in terms of the land area they cover (the world's largest banyan in India covers four acres), banyans spawn incredible roots. The Ringling grounds in Sarasota boasts fourteen banyans, and some are over one hundred years old. They drop roots from their branches, like multi-armed monsters, until one tree becomes a forest of hanging roots. As the tree ages, the stilt roots improve its stability by providing broader anchorage and support in unstable soil. The aerial roots also help the plant breathe. Like the mangroves, banyans become an ecological phenomenon, sustaining a vast variety of creatures.

These marvels of nature would fail without the roots that sustain, strengthen, and support them. Roots are the source of life—roots allow the banyans to breathe.

But what do *we* do when *our* grounders are ripped out? When someone we love dies, when divorce tears out family stability, when good health is not as strong as we thought? When our breathing is hampered and the things that make life breathable disappear. How do we survive and breathe when roots like these disappear?

These are not the roots that hold us in life's coastal hurricanes and twice-a-day tidal flooding. These are not the roots that support us in our aging, help us to become rich social and spiritual systems to enrich our world, sustain us in storms, and cause us to thrive in hostile environments. For roots like family and youth fade and die.

Like the mangroves and banyans, we will survive and thrive spiritually, relationally, and emotionally only as our roots grow deeper into the soil of God's love and forgiveness, as we remain connected to the tap root that gives us life.

These are deeper roots, roots that won't rot, weaken, or succumb to change and upheaval. Put down in the rich soil of faith, our roots, linked daily to God, to eternity, to purposes beyond our selfish desires, to divine fulfillment—these roots remain when all around us fails. Strong and tough like the mangroves. Stable and enduring like banyans.

A timely January trip to Florida was God's way of reminding me that my roots to youth and to generations of family here on Layton may disappear, but my roots in God's love, presence, and promises will remain strong and fruitful, even when and if I reach one hundred, even when tempests circle, for I am anchored in the shifting tides of life with Christ into eternity.

Yes, roots rule, and because of roots in Christ, we can breathe on Layton or wherever we walk.

Encouragement for Your Walk

"Blessed is the one who trusts in the Lord, whose confidence is in him. They will be like a tree planted by the water that sends out its roots by the stream. It does not fear when heat comes; its leaves are always green. It has no worries in a year of drought and never fails to bear fruit" (Jeremiah 17:7-8). Death, drought, divorce will never prevent us from putting our roots down more deeply into an anchored, rooted relationship with God, a relationship of trust, promise and breathability in the face of trials.

Lord, thank you for allowing us to root in You because of Jesus' sacrifice. Thank you that we do not have to sway and drown in the culture of our day, in false hopes, lies, and unkept promises. Strengthen our roots, our connection to You. Move us to spend time talking to you and studying your Word. Then, we will stand strong when flash floods of loss and pain threaten to overwhelm us. Grow our roots deeper daily in You and help us to breathe the air of the redeemed.

9. Refuge in the Rain

After a mid-winter snowstorm, rain assaulted our house on Layton.

Rain in January. An icy, damp, chilling, and generally depressing bit of weather.

At 3 p.m. the kitchen lights blazed in premature twilight. The kettle hissed on the stove, and I refilled my cup with another variety of Tazo. A week's worth of mail lay helter-skelter across the kitchen table. Bills, advertisements, late Christmas cards, early birthday cards, catalogs, a few large manila envelopes, even a package—the typical pile that awaits a vacationer upon her return from Christmas with the family three states away.

Rain pelted the kitchen window. Wind hurled the snow shovels across the porch, clattering and banging. Cracks and crannies in this old house admitted a chill.

I sorted the heap of mail carelessly, tossing fliers and ads on the floor, and randomly choosing to open any envelope that caught my eye.

There was a Christmas photo of my sister's family. Her annual holiday letter, always creative and lengthy, recounted the achievements of my niece and nephews through the past year. They had launched successfully from high school to college. I relished the list of accomplishments. News worth tweeting about.

I recognized Joan's broad, flourishing strokes on a card. We rarely see each other, but year after year, she never forgets to send a birthday wish. My birthday follows Christmas immediately, like a child afraid to be left behind. Increasingly, I wish it had been left behind a few years.

I opened several more birthday cards, some with small gifts tucked inside from friends separated by distance or long absence, and some from faithful friends nearby.

A yellow envelope, stuck with customs forms and the profile of Queen Elizabeth, could only be from cousin Ann in Wales, her annual holiday gift from the Celtic kingdom by the sea. One year she sent a Welsh cookbook. Another year a book of Welsh sayings. This year's souvenir—a CD of two Welsh tenors singing carols in their guttural, native language. Music of a distant time, with family ties, and ethereal satisfaction. It reminded me of my personal favorite among Welsh tenors—my grandfather.

I wanted to save the brown-papered box as the last piece of mail, but it wouldn't wait. Eddie's careful cursive and the San Francisco postmark called me. My translator during a visit to China fourteen years earlier, Eddie maintained our friendship. He left China during the ensuing years and came to live in America. The package captured the flavor of Frisco: a bag of Ghirardelli chocolates and a small ceramic horse, a reminder from Chinatown of the Year of the Horse.

I savored the observable presence of God at my kitchen table, and I stuffed a few of the Ghirardelli in my mouth, sipped a bit more Tazo, and enjoyed every minute of this gray-day-turned-sunshiny at my disheveled table.

This afternoon I knew God sat with me at that messy table in my rain-pelted house. His presence sang from each piece of mail. Love in one. Grace in another. Blessing in a third. The United States Postal Service deals in heavenly business.

God doesn't forget *birth*-days or ordinary days. He delights in showering us with blessings anytime. I sat indoors, awash in those rain showers. It was warm and sweet.

A final card, not meant for a birthday but heaped with blessing, simply left me breathless. Nestled inside was a gift that would pay for an entire year of "The Voice of Hope," our blog talk radio show into China.

That winter afternoon there was no outside world, no clattering on the porch, no concern about the mess on the table, just a kitchen aglow with His observable presence. HE filled the room. And I—I savored the beauty of basking in His love and attention while sitting in the rain.

Encouragement for Your Walk

STOP and ***S***avor ***T***he ***O***bservable ***P***resence of God on your road today, writes author Beth Moore.

Observe carefully small, daily things on the Walk, for God is always present as He was on our Emmaus Road, waiting for our eyes and hearts to acknowledge His presence. We should not allow the fears and uncertainties of the journey to distract and confuse us, for *"The Lord your God is with you, the Mighty Warrior who saves. He will take great delight in you, in his love he will no longer rebuke you, but will rejoice over you with singing"* (Zephaniah 3:17).

Part 3

The People We Meet

"As you walk through the valley of the unknown, you will find the footprints of Jesus both in front of you and beside you."

Charles Stanley,
Pastor, Television Evangelist, Author

10. People Matter

What can you learn in a school without computers, a core curriculum, or an anti-bullying policy? Plenty.

At least that was my conclusion as I considered the question in preparation for the fiftieth anniversary of our high school graduation.

The old gang has had a high school reunion every five years since we walked across the gym to "Pomp and Circumstance" in 1966. In fact, around the time of the fiftieth reunion, we decided to see each other more frequently as our ages increase and our numbers dwindle. We have added birthday parties to our five-year reunions for those mile marker birthday years— and, hopefully, will continue to do so into our nineties.

Remembrances of our country school those decades ago are dragged regularly out of memory mothballs, shaken free of cobwebs, and hung up to laugh about.

Our alma mater, Scott School, in the country hollow called Montdale, was a one story, rectangular building with a single hallway down its center, spilling off into classrooms on either side. In 1953 the class of '66 started kindergarten at one end of the building, and each year we worked our way up the hallway, classroom to classroom, until thirteen years later when we reached the other end of the building where an exit door marked the way into the great beyond.

We should have been overcome with fear and intimidation on June 6, 1966, when we left our school for the last time. After all, President Kennedy had been assassinated when we were in ninth grade. The Vietnam War broiled and escalated daily, and soon a lottery draft would call more of our boys across the world into military service. The South rumbled with civil rights marches, and in two years Dr. King would be shot. The '60s seethed anxiety, cultural change, and social upheaval, and we were stepping right into the thick of it. But in June 1966, we were eighteen, cocooned, and clueless in our mountain country school.

If you grew up on Layton Road in the 40s, 50s or 60s, the old Scott School became a second home.

In the midst of a complex world of national and international turmoil, our school was simple: We didn't have computers, cell phones, printers, or video games. Of course, these hadn't been invented yet. Our valued possession in '66 might have been our transistor radios. If you needed to call home, you had to ask Francis, the school secretary, to use the office phone.

We didn't have a cafeteria or a library. We took lunch boxes and then bag lunches every day for thirteen years and ate at our desks. The locker room was in the basement. One classroom was held in the scary down-under, accessible only over boards laid on the basement's dirt floor.

We didn't have football, soccer, track, or cross country.

We didn't have well-paid teachers. When I started teaching in 1970, my starting salary was seven thousand dollars, so who knows what our teachers were paid in the fifties and sixties.

We didn't have a science lab, but Miss Santacroce and Mr. Vail did their best with a few beakers and a flip chart of plants.

We didn't have new textbooks. In fact, the list of users on the inside front covers of our books extended back a decade or so.

We didn't have creative teaching supplies and resources—like posters.

What we lacked forms a dismal and negative list, but that's just part of the story. Despite the frugality and the "it was different in my day" attitude, none of the "didn't have's," none of the world tension, seemed to bother my classmates. In fact, the thirty-six of us were a happy bunch.

After all...

We had Donnie. A victim of polio, the scourge of childhood in the fifties, Donnie had a large hump on his back that prevented him from standing straight. In fact, he couldn't stand on his own at all. He used crutches throughout our school years, dragging his deformed foot that was far beyond normal size. But he kept up with us in every activity, even our five-day trip to Washington DC. He smiled continuously. The boys included him in every event, even as a stat keeper at basketball games. In all our school years, I don't remember any teacher lecturing us on how to treat Donnie or reprimanding us for bullying him. He was our friend. The whole class showed up at the funeral when Donnie died the year after graduation, his entire life encompassed in that little country school. Donnie taught us that people in that big outside world would be different from us, but they were one with us.

We had Rosemarie. A newcomer to the school in tenth grade, Rosemarie quickly became my best friend. Although my classmates and I had been together for many years, they immediately included the new girl with her marvelous sense of humor and happy disposition. A foster child at Stillmeadow, a home for many foster children, Rosemarie didn't tell us the story of her family or how she came to foster care. But even at the age of fifteen, she showed us how to make the best of things, whatever heartache life threw her way. Rosemarie left Scott for Penn State University. From her we learned how to laugh in the face of adversity and how to work hard to reverse our futures.

We had Patti with her syrupy Southern accent. Her parents moved to Pennsylvania from North Carolina to work at a local Bible camp. Patti carried her Bible to school every day. Everyone in the class came from a church-going family, the Catholics attending Corpus Christi and the Protestants attending Mt. Bethel or the Primitive Baptist in Justus, or the United Methodist church in Montdale. But Patti's commitment to Jesus missed us. She wasn't just a church attender. She would read her Bible in study halls or at lunch. It would be about ten years after high school when I would begin a personal relationship with Jesus when I met Him on my Emmaus Road. Patti had a relationship with Jesus which eluded me in high school, despite my upbringing.

No one ever ridiculed Patti. She was part of our group. She earned our respect through her diligent academic work and her faithful love for God. She was rewarded as class valedictorian. From Patti we learned about commitment to God and the courage to live it in front of her peers.

We had Evelyn and Billy. Their school romance began early in ninth grade. Neither of them even looked at or dated anyone else through high school. Truly, their eyes were only for each other. A month after we graduated in July of '66, they were married. The summer we celebrated our fiftieth reunion, they also celebrated their fiftieth wedding anniversary. Many of us in the class faced divorce through the years, but Billy and Evelyn plodded on, fighting cancer, building a business, rearing three children. From Bill and Evelyn, we learned the importance of faithfulness and commitment in relationships.

Our class produced company owners, a nurse practitioner, several teachers, sales managers, leaders in large area companies, a pastor, several professors, an academic doctor, an airline stewardess, hairdressers, bankers, a massage therapist, a bevy of marvelous mothers and fathers, and an entire class of responsible, hard-working people of character who raised families, paid taxes, and helped to form the backbone of America.

In a recent letter Patti wrote to me, "Considering all the things we didn't have, I think we got a pretty good education. It surely isn't about how much money is spent or how much technology is available per student that determines the quality of education."

In hindsight and from the vantage point of a Christian, I can see God's fingerprints all over our thirteen years in the Scott School. God blessed us in our early, formative years with friendships, adults who loved us, and a safe environment. God's special blessing to the class of '66 at Scott School was a protected environment to grow and loving relationships. God gave us a bedrock start on life, unsullied by the craziness of the 1960s. None of us fell through the cracks. God's watchful care has followed us these nearly sixty years, whether we choose to acknowledge it or not. He is always there.

How much richer would our teen years and our school experience have been if we recognized His presence back then and lived each day for His glory? But now, with an Emmaus Road meeting and acceptance of Jesus, the landscape behind us is forgiven and sweetened, a source of unrecognized blessings. And the landscape ahead is richer and fuller with our knowledge of our future home in heaven

What can you learn in a school without computers, a core curriculum, and an anti-bullying policy?

Plenty, my friends. Plenty.

Encouragement for Your Walk

"The Lord will keep you from all harm—he will watch over your life; the Lord will watch over your coming and going both now and forevermore" (Psalm 121:7-8). Every step of our journey, God's love and watch care surround us, even though we may be oblivious to it. God pointed me to an unexpected career path in college, one I had never considered, because He knew what I would need on the road up ahead. I was not seeking or following Him at the time, but He watched my ways and led me. How many times in those years, when I gave no obeisance to God, did He rescue me, and how many more times did He allow me to suffer the pain of my wrong choices to teach me and lead me to Him?

Lord, we ask commitment and devotion to you for our friends and families. Turn their hearts to you and keep them from wandering aimlessly at the whims of the culture. We pray they will know your holiness, their sinfulness, your sufficiency and their need of you to walk the road.

11. Reach Out and Touch

Le Bron James, star of the Cleveland Cavaliers in 2014, met Prince William and his wife Kate when they attended his NBA game against the Brooklyn Nets. In a typically American gesture of friendliness and familiarity, LeBron put his arm around the shoulder of Princess Kate, the future queen of England.

The result was a collective gasp from the British media, a gasp heard round the world. "British media has its knickers in a bunch," said the Mercury News Network. How dare LeBron presume to touch the nation's treasure.

"According to protocol in Britain, a commoner is not supposed to touch members of the royal family, even if it is an innocent gesture," chimed the *Huffington Post*. Americans have become infamous for breaching the "no touch" rule, the *Post* affirmed, citing a *faux pas* of Michelle Obama who put her arm on Queen Elizabeth II's back during a 2009 visit to Buckingham Palace.

"Invading the personal space of others is practically an American duty," wrote Tony Hicks for the Mercury News.

News Flash: God touches us. Divine royalty touches humanity. In startling juxtaposition to the protocol, traditions, and expectations of the British monarchy stands the King of the universe, God, whose kingdom encompasses the British Empire and all kingdoms to the outer reaches of our galaxy and beyond. God—the King of all kings.

This King entered our physical realm one night in a dirty stable, in a non-descript town, in a distant part of our world. He entered the world as a baby who needed to be touched and cuddled. He entered our space because He *wanted* us to touch the one true and living God.

There is no protocol about keeping a safe distance from the Holy of Holies. No concerns about maintaining a respectful distance. The "no touch" rule of the world's monarchies did not exist for God. His goal was to be up close and personal with His created people. To touch and be touched.

On Christmas we celebrate His birth, His stepping into touch-ability, accessibility. "Come close," He whispered.

The good news: God in human form, Jesus, took the ultimate step in closing the space between us. He sacrificed Himself on a cross, and with that one act He provided the forgiveness that would forever eliminate the gap between the Creator God and His creation. Accepting His sacrifice drew us to Him—with no separation. The unfathomable, untouchable God became Christ in us. Distance was forever dispersed.

He became Emmanuel, God with us, God in us, God forever walking in touchable nearness to us.

We rub shoulders with thousands of people in a lifetime on our Walk. How do we touch them with the kindness, love, or patience of God? Simple words touch and encourage others. "Great job!" "You are an excellent waitress." "Billy, I'm so proud of how well you are doing in school." "Thanks for helping with the dishes." Fix a single mom's broken doorknob. Bake brownies for the elderly man across the street. Call a friend struggling with a broken arm. Deliver a pile of groceries to the local homeless shelter. Most of our fellow travelers labor through their days, burdened and beaten by life. Simple acts or words of encouragement spark life and gratefulness. Even a sincere smile can lift someone's spirit and change the course of the day. How are you "touching" those on your road with God's compassion?

Whatever our futures may hold, know that God longs to be near us, to touch us with His love, to comfort us in our pain, direct us in our indecision, or lift us in our depression. His royalty does not preclude His love. Seek to walk in the shadow of His nearness and to pass His kindness to whomever you meet.

Encouragement for Your Walk

"Watch what God does, and then you do it, like children who learn proper behavior from their parents. Mostly what God does is love you. Keep company with him and learn a life of love…" (Ephesians 5:1-2a, *The Message*). Learn from God how to touch those on your journey with love. He asks us to be kind to one another and tender-hearted. These "touches" will leave indelible impressions and shine a light on His goodness. Walk with others in touchable nearness as God walks with you.

Lord, we long for Your loving touch, Your comfort and closeness, especially when the road is rough. But help us to live large, to shift the focus to our fellow travelers and not suffocate ourselves. Make us aware of needs and give us the love and energy to touch others with your love.

12. The Old Dirt Road

Roads connect. They give us access to other places, other people. They can be a lifeline to a vital destination or a way to escape. Jesus walked the Calvary Road, a road forever etched in our minds as a heart rending, blood-bathed terminus. But with God, all roads can be rerouted, all directions can be changed.

The actual story of Layton Road, not its metaphorical and symbolic Walk with God, came to life, as most roads do, through years of development and service to its community. Development and service—integral factors in our growing relationship with God.

Howard Detty's story finds its roots in the creation of the community that grew up along Layton.

The Works Progress Administration (WPA) came to our farming village of Justus during Franklin D. Roosevelt's administration, bringing authentic road status to the cow path that was Layton Road. The WPA employed a large number of men in its construction. They worked throughout the winter to build the road that was purported to cost only five thousand dollars a mile. Howard Detty, an old friend of my grandmother's, remembers how hard the men worked and their dire poverty as they labored with raw fingers, barren of even gloves, during the most bitter cold.

Howard might be dubbed one of the "tap roots," if not one of the "founding fathers," of our small village, Justus, one of the "pavers" of Layton Road.

Eventually, Howard began to build homes as the construction of

Layton brought a burgeoning population to Justus. At first, they were small Cape Cod style homes which he sold for a few thousand dollars. Later, the houses he built were large three-bedroom ranches that are still some of the finest houses in Justus. One of his last ranch houses sold for about twenty-five thousand dollars sixty years ago. Recently, that same home was resold by its owner for over two-hundred-fifty thousand dollars. Undoubtedly, his favorite house was the one he built across from the old family homestead where he cared for his mother until her death in her late nineties. It continued to be his residence until the end of his life.

Although Howard had no children of his own, he was a friend and mentor to many young people through the years. He qualifies for the name "Patriarch of Justus." The weight and burden of the title for him is in watching so many of his contemporaries pass on. "I've counted over a hundred people on Layton Road who were my friends and have died," he said.

In 2010 when my three-year-old granddaughter Anna visited my house on Layton Road in Justus, she came to a busy community, a far century's cry from the quiet farm village of Mr. Detty's birth in 1913. Howard was instrumental in bringing about the change, having built over forty homes on or near Layton and having served as a bulwark of the community's fabric and foundation for nearly one hundred years.

In 1913 Woodrow Wilson sat in the White House and the suffragettes marched in Washington D.C. for the right to vote, but Justus, hardly a speck on the map, nestled between several mountains, was removed from the tumult of change and the brewing winds of World War I. Eugene and Julia Detty, Howard's parents, were living in Julia Ackerley Detty's family homestead, a saltbox style house on Layton Road which has been renovated, and, at over one-hundred-sixty years old, continues to be used today as a family home. It was one of the few houses in the heart of Justus at that time. Today, Justus boasts Corky's Garden Path as its geographic center, but in 1913 Layton Road itself was a garden path.

Howard remembers travelling with his father on a horse-drawn wagon to Mifflin Street in Scranton which was a gathering place for country farmers to market their produce. In addition to other crops, the Dettys would plant over an acre of strawberries each year. Until he was about ninety, Howard continued to cultivate and sell his berries at a stand in front of his new home—everything sold "on your honor" in the front yard.

Although Howard's father used farming to supplement the family income, his primary job was as a bookkeeper for one of the valley coal mines. Like other Justus residents who were riding the economic boom of the coal mining era, Howard's father Eugene would walk over the mountain each day to the mine offices in the valley. One of Howard's most vivid memories was of his father who had been beaten up by union miners who had mistaken him as a "scab," crossing their picket lines.

Another traumatic family memory involved Howard's Grandmother Emily Ackerley's first husband who was killed in the Civil War. The letter from an officer, informing the family of his death, remains among Howard's treasured family possessions. Farming, mining, and the Civil War trace the family's history and reflect the pattern of late nineteenth and early twentieth century America on Layton Road.

Life was difficult for early 20th century inhabitants of Justus. In fact, when asked about his preference for the early years or the modern conveniences of Justus, Howard did not succumb to nostalgia but unequivocally advocated the joys of the twenty-first century. "It was just too hard back then," he remarked. Indoor plumbing was unheard of, and even a drink of water involved winding up a bucket from the well in the Detty's backyard.

Transportation was problematic. Layton Road itself was nothing but two ruts, "muddy all year and narrow as wagon wheels" which were able to "rip the sides off the tires" of the early vehicles that tried to navigate its distance. "I'll never forget the sight of Stanley White marching his herd of cows up the road," Howard reminisced as he watched a string of quitting-time vehicles zoom up Layton, oblivious to the former cow-path status of their home route. Howard also remembered his mother walking regularly from Justus to Chinchilla, a three-mile downhill trek with an incredible return trip incline, to get a trolley that would take her to Scranton and the markets.

Like the other early residents of Justus, Howard attended a one-room schoolhouse on Justus Corners called, simply, the Justus School. All ages through eighth grade were educated in this one small building which stood on Justus Corners until about 2019. The children of Justus were not educated beyond the eighth grade until the Scott School was built in Montdale and they were able to acquire a high school diploma. By that time Howard felt that it was too late for him to go back to school, so he opted to drive the first school bus, transporting Justus children over the mountain to the Scott School after the one-room schoolhouse closed. His career as a school bus driver spanned several generations from the 1930s to the early 1960s.

Justus has been blessed to have citizens like Howard Detty in its history. His friendships have spanned generations; his kindness and generosity are legendary. If there is a heartbeat at the center of Justus, it must reside with Howard—on Layton.

What road encompasses your daily life? Do you know your neighbors? Do you walk life in community or isolation and uninvolvement? Layton or Lakefield, Eastview Drive or Poor Farm Road, these are the places we live and serve, the places we allow God's presence to be seen and felt by passersby. What spiritual legacy are you leaving on your Layton?

Encouragement for Your Walk

Our lives are peppered with people, some right in our backyards, who are sacrificially loved by God—but don't know it. Some may walk the whole distance of their life road without the forgiveness, purpose, and future God promises. Some may even die with no recognition of their Creator who provided an iron-clad promise of entrance into heaven because of the sacrifice of His Son Jesus. Tragic, empty living that always ends in a grave.

Take an Emmaus Road Walk with the God you do not know. Seek Him. Talk to others who know Him. Find the One who will fill the void and point you Home. Let Him help you to carry your burdens, for our roads are pot-holed with ruts that can "rip the sides off your tires."

God of the universe and God of our small communities, draw our people to you. Give them a glimpse of eternity. May our Walk with you be so deeply rooted in doing your will and walking your way that the fruits of your Spirit in us, kindness, generosity, and faithfulness, will spill all over other people and our world. Keep us walking your road—faithfully.

13. Strangers We See

The siren song of travel sang its sweet melody to me again from my winter hibernation to points near Scranton and Wilkes Barre. No bathing suits, no sunshine, no aircraft or taxi.

For travel's glory is not only the monuments and mountains of foreign soil. It is people—their food, traditions, music, language, and culture. By this definition, travel can happen even to our local city where coal was king—if foreigners are involved.

And foreigners were the prime focus of my local travel adventure.

First stop, Marywood College for "Conversation Corner" with English language learners from around the world who are studying at the college. My job entailed talking—that simple. Allow our foreign friends to practice and speak English through lengthy conversations with native English speakers. Afternoon conversations with two Marywood students took me to Asia and the Middle East.

My first conversation partner was Zhicheng Zhang (also called Frank). Frank came to the U.S. just two months before. "Fresh off the boat," eager, and enthusiastic about all things American, he chose to speak to me, instead, of his home in China. Perhaps he had been in America long enough to miss his Chinese meals, his family, and his home. In our imaginations we walked through the streets of Beijing as Frank practiced his English, and I stumbled through some Mandarin. Frank spoke of dinners with his friends that ended at midnight, of large bowls of bok choy and fish, of roaming Beijing's streets with his buddies and snacking at street vendors' wagons. He remembered Spring Festival holidays when he and his family traveled to exotic places in the west of China, like Kunming. I hoped this nostalgic opportunity to speak of home allayed his homesickness. A foreign college student in America doesn't only need practice with the language. They need friends. Frank and I took a step in the door of friendship that afternoon.

Frank's studies in health care at Marywood would prepare him to return to China to "help his country."

Without the aid of technology or transportation, I left China and moved to another conversation table in the room, travelling thousands of miles to a Middle Eastern country. Unlike most international travel, my destination would be a surprise. Another new friend awaited at the next table. Mr. Mohammad came to America from Kurdistan-Iraq, which seemed more foreign to me than China where I had spent considerable time. Although I will probably never get to visit Kurdistan-Iraq, Mr. Mohammed brought the country he loves to Northeast Pennsylvania through our conversation time.

He, his wife, and children came to the U.S. several years before, long enough for the family to ache for the way of life they knew back home. His voice cracked as he reminisced about relatives, his home, the city, meals with his extended family, the wild activity of the streets, and the food. Food aroused the most nostalgia for these foreign friends. Family, friends, and relationships happened around food. It is the Eastern way.

God's Word, the Bible, is set in the Eastern culture. A cultural norm, Jesus and his disciples experienced their most intimate moments around meals. They would recline at table, ready to spend as much time as necessary to connect with those around them. At the Passover meal in the upper room on the night before Jesus was crucified, his friends witnessed at the table what would happen the following day, as He broke and offered them the bread of life: His body would be given in sacrifice. It would be broken for their sins. The meal would be their Last Supper together on this side of heaven. Frank and Mr. Mohammed would understand the value of long and intimate meals together. Perhaps this ritual motivated their desires to return home.

Mr. Mohammed's goal in the US was to obtain a master's degree in public administration. Like Frank, his ambition was to go back and help his country. Mohammed and his family would return to Kurdistan at the end of the year to work for his government. War-torn and beleaguered, the Kurds had fought bravely for their country against Muslim extremists. My first Kurdish friend left me with a sweet taste of the courage, strength, and character of the people of Kurdistan-Iraq and an appreciation for those who sacrifice the comforts of the home they know to travel around the world and gain an education to benefit the lives of those in their own countries.

An avid traveler himself, Mark Twain once said, "Travel is fatal to prejudice, bigotry, and narrow-mindedness." May I amend your thought, Mr. Twain? "Even befriending people in our neighborhoods who come from around the world is fatal to prejudice, bigotry, and narrow-mindedness." Our world seethes war and strife. What can one person do to make a difference in such a world, especially when travel to some countries is impossible? I suggest that the way to make a difference in the world is to make friends with the foreigners in our own backyards.

That afternoon at Marywood College with new friends from China and Kurdistan, *sans* jet lag and luggage, impressed on me the importance of reaching out to people of other nationalities right here in the USA. The adjustment to American life could not be easy.

Scripture reminds us of the population of heaven, *"I saw a huge crowd, too huge to count. Everyone was there—all nations and tribes, all races and languages"* (Revelation 7:9, *The Message*).

On our journeys an outstretched hand, a listening ear, or a pot of soup will begin a friendship—a good and godly purpose for our life Walk. Befriend the foreign family in the supermarket or the dollar store. Translate for them or read the prices and signs to them. Our cities abound with people from other countries. Perhaps, the friendship will open the door for you to share the love of the One with whom you walk—a worthy goal and purpose.

I traveled continents in one week, and the only expense was a Chinese buffet for a Spring Festival celebration with Chinese friends in Wilkes Barre. I experienced countries because I experienced people. God is in the business of people.

Henry Miller, an American novelist, wrote, "My destination was not a place, but it was a new way of seeing things."

Encouragement for Your Walk

God's invitation into relationship with Him extends to every nation, tribe, people and language. Our Creator God seeks all people for He has created them and by His will they exist. He involves us in giving His invitation to the world. His mandate to us is called the Great Commission: *"...go and make disciples of all nations, baptizing them in the name of the Father and of the Son and of the Holy Spirit, and teaching them to obey everything I have commanded you. And surely, I am with you always, to the very end of the age"* (Matthew 28:19-20).

On your Walk this purpose for living looms large. To whom can you give God's invitation? To someone of another race, language, or nation? To someone in your neighborhood, at work, in the grocery store? God has given us a mission and purpose.

Lord, empower us to relate to all people in our sphere of influence and beyond as the precious, well-loved, recipients of God's grace.

Part 4
Paths of Purpose

*"We have the presence and promises of God.
We are meant to march to that great music"* ...
*"True valor lies, not in what the world calls success,
but in the dogged going on when everything in the man
says Stop."*

Amy Carmichael
Christian missionary in India for 55 years

14. Who's Got Talent?

In the fall of 1953, America was entering a new era that would revolutionize the world. A technology revolution swept the country that would change American culture and the world forever: Television. Between September and November that fall of '53, over forty television channels began operation in cities across the United States. Television and the baby boomers would come of age together.

Justus, our country village on a mountain in Pennsylvania, had never been on the cutting edge of technology, or anything else for that matter, but here on Layton that fall of '53, our family was on the cusp of the national communication development. We owned a television, probably one of the first families on Layton to move the oversized electronic device with a lilliputian screen and giant tubes into the corner of our living room.

With its black and white pictures, it housed a wild assortment of wires and tubes in a marvelous array of shapes, sizes, and colors. And my Dad was tube and television savvy, thanks to the United States Army and anthracite.

After World War II and his discharge from the army in 1945, Dad returned to his parents' home in Justus and took up the family occupation, coal mining. His father and Uncle Joe, trained in the mines of North Wales, brought their skills and manpower to our local valley mines. One of the relatives found Dad a job at the breaker in Olyphant. From the war front in Italy to the coal mines in northeastern Pennsylvania, it was a bleak and black decade for Dad.

THE WALK ON LAYTON

He knew before a year was up that coal would not be his future. To his credit, he took the coal car by its hitch and sought out a better way of life. The post-World War II economy in the U.S. was beginning to sing, and innovations and inventions were changing American life. Dad jumped off the coal breaker and took advantage of his army training in communications by pursuing a burgeoning career field that did not involve dodging enemies or groveling underground in mines—television engineering. In the late forties and early fifties, it was *the* place to be for a young vet with Morse Code in his head and electricity in his blood, even if he lived on a mountain in the country on a road called Layton.

Television had a rough start. Poor Philo Farnsworth produced the first electronic television picture in 1927 and, by rights, he should have been hailed as the inventor of television, but he was scooped by RCA in a patent battle. Because RCA's David Sarnoff successfully marketed the invention, he became known as the father of television. The old "squeaky wheel" got the credit and the attention. Philo died in obscurity although with a label like Philo he'd have probably had to choose a power name to make it in modern TV. It wasn't until the 1939 World's Fair, when RCA unveiled their new NBC Studios at Rockefeller Plaza in New York, that network television was introduced.

Television's commercial success and growth languished when the U.S. entered WW II as the work force shipped overseas, and personnel were scarce. But in 1947 with the war behind them and an army of young veterans back in the states, television exploded. Dad rode the wave.

He took his post-war bride, Annette, and enrolled in the American Television Institute of Technology (ATIT) in Chicago. They loaded up the Plymouth and began the grueling drive across Route 6 in Pennsylvania through Ohio and Indiana to Illinois and a one room walk-up apartment on the south side of the Windy City.

Founded by Dr. Lee DeForest, inventor of the vacuum tube, and U.A. Sanabria, developer of the first television station, ATIT was home for the country's cutting-edge training in television theory, manufacturing, operation, and development.

Dad studied all aspects of electronics and television technology while Mom put her nursing education to work at Woodlawn Hospital. We went back to Chicago in 1991 to locate the apartment, the school, and the hospital. The hospital had been leveled, and an empty plot marked its former location. Boarded and broken windows, metal gates on store fronts, and litter under the "EL" (elevated train) indicated that the apartment building had slipped into the slums. And the school—well, televisions had come a long way from vacuum tubes.

During the four years they lived near Lake Michigan, Dad finished his education, and in 1949 the young couple had their first baby, a girl. Dad was able to leave Chicago with a Bachelor of Science degree in television engineering and a small family. One coal miner had made a significant move to better his life. The young family headed home to the hills of Pennsylvania. Dad would find a job with one of the first radio stations in Scranton, WGBI, and later with one of its first television stations, WDAU (later WYOU).

Smart and creative, Dad set the bar for success high. A background of poverty, immigration, war, backbreaking work in the mines—none of those challenges kept Dad from pushing on and doing his best. I never remember him as a complainer, even when the main beam in the basement was termite-ridden and he had to replace it himself. Or when the basement filled with three inches of water after a broken sump pump and it had to be cleaned. Dad worked hard until his death near the age of ninety-nine and he left my sons, my sisters, and me with an example of what it means to do our best for God and to do it with whole-hearted passion.

Talents and skills are the gifts of a generous Creator. God's gifts for our Walk empower us to serve others and to bring purpose to our days. When used for the glory of God, talents and skills shine a spotlight on Him.

Dad's skills inspired our family. He could build a house, wire it for electricity, and repair anything faulty from broken water pipes to a recalcitrant furnace. His artwork had the children continually asking, "Can you draw a horse, a house, mommy, etc.?" And his powerful tenor voice made him an in-demand part of barbershop quartets and church choirs. At ninety he could out-distance most seventy-year-olds on the walking trail. Dad was gifted, and he recognized his gifts as a holy calling to honor God and serve others. Like most talented people, those gifts required grooming and training.

Dad didn't quote mottos for living, but as I watched him through my seventieth year, I witnessed him live one of the primary disciplines of the Walk with God: *"Whatever you do, work at it with all your heart, working for the Lord, not for human masters, since you know that you will receive an inheritance from the Lord as a reward. It is the Lord Christ you are serving"* (Colossians 3:23). Dad's diligence and hard work remain my model for a Walk that pleases God.

Dad walked his own Emmaus Road into the forties and fifties, but when he turned his life over to Jesus, his strong work ethic, kindness, and love for Jesus created in Him a servant's heart, a heart God had prepared in advance. Every day of his journey he worked heartily—fixing a light or ceiling tiles for one of us, building a porch for another, installing an intercom system for a third. Every neighbor Dad ever had leaned into his kindness and servant heart—and into his carpentry and fix-it skills. Dad walked his Layton world with a hammer and screwdriver and a driving desire to do whatever God asked of him.

Many rewards will grace the life of one with a servant heart who works heartily unto the Lord and not unto men. Seek to use your skills for the people on your path.

*Resource: *The Archive of American Television* http://www.emmytvlegends.org/resources/tv-history, Accessed January 27, 2016.

Encouragement for Your Walk

"Each of you should use whatever gift you have received to serve others, as faithful stewards of God's grace in its various forms ... If anyone serves, they should do so with the strength God provides, so that in all things God may be praised through Jesus Christ" (1 Peter 4:10-11).

Do you seek to serve those around you and to give your best at the job God has given you? Do you give one hundred percent because you are actually working for God, not your employer? Or is complaining an important part of your workday?

The discipline of service on our Christian Walk is a strong testimony to the presence and action of God in our lives. We should work and serve for His glory, not our own. On our bumpy roads when troubles abound and the going gets rough, revert to the discipline of hard work. Becoming entrenched in a job for Jesus will transform focus and purpose.

Father, you are a working God…You spent six days creating before you rested. Please give us the energy and strength to keep going and to do our best, especially when our strength fails. Thank you for the examples of family and friends who never flagged in their desire to serve and work for You. Help us to live as servants on our Walk.

15. Marching in Armor

Two small knights waged war in my backyard.

Riding stick horses and wearing plastic helmets and breastplates as armor, my grandsons galloped around their kingdom. Brandishing wooden swords at trees, yard chairs, and even the cat, they brought all to submission. Their war whoops declared the bravery of stout-hearted men marching to victory.

"Oh, Lord," I prayed, "let this be the courage these boys demonstrate as they follow you in their own Walk through life's battles. Give them an armor-bearing friend and brother."

Two young men of ancient days in the Bible displayed this confident courage. Jonathan and his armor-bearer set out alone to attack the Philistines in the pass at Mikmash. The armor-bearer must have known Jonathan well, for in the face of overwhelming odds, he trusted his God-honoring mentor, declaring his willingness to do whatever Jonathan had in mind and to follow him with his heart and soul. God gave these young men victory and twenty Philistines were killed.

"Do all that you have in mind', his (Jonathon's) armor-bearer said. 'Go ahead. I am with you heart and soul'" (1 Samuel 14:7). If a soldier must enter battle, who wouldn't want an armor-bearer with a conviction to stick with you, no matter what happened? A friend in the lunchroom or the boardroom or the classroom or the battlefield. We want someone to have our backs, preferably with armor.

Paul encourages us in Ephesians 6:11 to *"Put on the full armor of God, so we can take our stand against the devil's schemes."* We are admonished to be clad in the belt of truth, the breastplate of righteousness, the shield of faith, the helmet of salvation, and the sword of the Spirit.

Fitted with this armor, we face our daily skirmishes on the Walk.

Chances are we may never be called upon to step into an actual battle, and armor has given way to technology and protection of a different sort. But the reality is, we will see battle—perhaps on a daily basis. Our battle is against immorality, deceit, anger, bitterness, evil of every sort. How do we stand strong on our Walk when we are beset on every side with arrows of assault and pain?

Like Jonathan's armor-bearer, we can stand when we rest in complete trust in God's love, faithfulness, and sovereignty. With trust and faith, we can whisper, "Do all you have in mind, Lord. Go ahead of me into this battle. I am with you heart and soul."

God promises that when the day of battle comes, we will be able to *stand* our ground against the enemy, and He will be there with us, our faithful King and Protector.

The plastic helmets and wooden swords of our human efforts can be discarded for the power of God in us. Onward we march, arrayed in His armor of protective promises to whatever lies ahead on our journey.

Encouragement for Your Walk

The scent of war, brewing on our Walk, raises our apprehension and fears. The worst may happen. We see it in family discord, divorce, teenage rebellion, fatal diseases—war. Sin runs amuk in our families and in our world. Theft, murder, sexual immorality, slander, lying, deceit, and foolishness abound.

Because we live in a world beset by sin, we will suffer the consequences of our own or someone else's sin during the long Walk home. Like the boys in my yard, we must put on God's armor to protect ourselves and to withstand sin in our lives and not fall. Without God's divine protective shield, we are powerless. A Jonathon-friend who promises to encourage us in the daily face-offs against evil and to "have our backs" is God's way of giving hands and feet to His presence.

Lord, may we be faithful in submissively donning the armor of your Word and standing on your promises against the sin that runs rampant about us. You are with us, but our hearts sink and we tremble. We need you, Lord. Without you, we fail. Etch this reminder in our hearts, *"No, in all these things we are more than conquerors through Him who loved us. For I am convinced that neither death nor life, neither angels or demons, neither the present nor the future, nor any power, neither height nor depth, nor anything else in all creation, will be able to separate us from the love of God that is in Christ Jesus our Lord"* (Romans 8:37-39).

16. Purposeful Paths

Our health care professionals and first-responders lived grueling, dangerous days battling COVID-19 while saving and protecting lives. No question about it: they had purpose, motivation, goals, *ikigai*, or purpose for living.

"A reason to get out of bed in the morning, something that makes life worth living" is a rough translation of the Japanese word *ikigai*. The French call it *raison d'etre*. In America, thanks to Rick Warren's book, we call it *The Purpose-Driven Life*.

Whether we are on the frontlines of a medical crisis, in a world conflagration, entrenched in cultural or personal turmoil, or retired and facing long, lonely days at home, we all need an *ikigai* to walk our Layton roads.

So, what's your *ikigai*?

Times like a quarantine can try the spirits of the hardiest among us. Without an *ikigai*, our days can be empty and meaningless.

Extra time on your hands and isolation may have you wondering, "What on earth am I here for?" Days passed without marker events to delineate them and often without any motivation. A life without purpose is an empty life. "It's motion without meaning, activity without direction, and events without reason," Rick Warren writes.

National Geographic ran a story in 2005 on areas of the world with the greatest longevity. Okinawa, Japan, had one of the highest concentrations of people over one-hundred-years-old. The demographic study revealed that one of the top lifestyle reasons for their longevity was the individual's sense of life purpose, their *ikigai*.

What's your reason for getting out of bed during days of isolation, turmoil, stress, and trouble? What's your reason to keep walking? To enrich the lives of your children? To improve some else's life? To foster closer family relationships? To serve a neighbor? Purposes that look beyond ourselves to those around us may not increase our bank accounts or even our own pleasure, but other-centered purposes are life's most rewarding goals.

When we reach the end of our days and look back on our lives, will we be remembered because we finished our bucket list and did every thing we could to make ourselves happy? Or will we be remembered because the primary goal of our lives was to bring help and joy into the lives of others and, in so doing, to serve God?

God often works in paradigms. When we set serving others as our *ikigai*, the joy of giving comes right back to us.

"For such a time as this" was the reason given for Queen Esther's appearance before the king in order to save her people. Even though precedent and history assured her she would probably be killed, Esther chose to sacrifice herself, if necessary, for the good of her people.

Perhaps it is "for such a time as this" that we are living through war, social unrest, addictions, family breakups. Our lives are not demanded of us, as they may be for some police, military, and health care workers, but "purpose" certainly is. When we get out of bed each day, let's creatively imagine what we can do from our isolation, stress, or pain to make life a bit better for someone else on our Walk.

Here are a few ideas to change someone's day:

- Offer to make a prescription or grocery run for the elderly or handicapped in your neighborhood or social circle. Do they have any spring or fall yard chores you could do to help? Or a driveway to clear of snow?
- Cards or notes are a welcome sight when we open the mailbox. Even with texting and emailing, a card can go a long way to brighten someone's day. Send lots.

brighten someone's day. Send lots.
- Let your kitchen be a boon to someone: bake cookies, make soup, or a casserole. How fun to leave a treat on someone's porch. No need to even go to the door. Just text, "Check your porch."
- Pick up a few spring plants and leave them at the doors of people you want to encourage.
- Call or text friends, relatives, neighbors regularly. Some people who live alone may not have anyone checking in on them. Make it a "must-do" to text your children and grandchildren regularly.
- Donate to a local food bank or another organization that helps the needy.
- Give a grocery store gift card to a needy family.
- Tip a grocery store worker or any one of our "necessary" helpers for serving you. Tips might include a "Well done. Good job. Thank you."
- Order a pizza or take-out meal from a local restaurant for someone.
- ZOOM out-of-town family members.

Whatever our personal stress, the state of the world, the condition of the government, or the trouble in our homes, looking beyond ourselves to others and seeking to cultivate the highest purpose for living by serving will shift our focus and lift our spirits. Consider cultivating each day a servant's attitude, a higher reason for putting one foot in front of the other on your Walk.

Encouragement for Your Walk

Jen Wilkin, a nationally known women's Bible teacher, calls this deeper obedience, "the ministry of the more than halfway," referring to Matthew 5:41: *"If anyone forces you to go one mile, go with them two miles."* Making an impact on our culture involves standing out in the crowd, doing what they would not expect in kindness and generosity, responding counter intuitively to our culture with Christ's love.

Lord, help us to see a need and meet it. Let our journey be other-focused rather than self-indulged. Empower us to live open-handed. Thank you for blessing us in ways that allow us to bless others.

17. Artists in Kindness

Ca' d'Zan Mansion, the dazzling palatial home of John and Mable Ringling of Ringling Circus fame, stands in regal splendor on Sarasota Bay in Florida. John Ringling's Museum of Art flanks his mansion. It contains his personal collection of masterpieces featuring paintings and sculptures by the great Old Masters including Rubens, Titian, El Greco, van Dyck, and Gainsborough. A replica of the Greek statue *David* by Michelangelo, as well as Italian fountains and a bay front terrace of marble in mosaic patterns, further grace the grounds. The Ringling complex of mansion, museum, courtyards, rose gardens, banyan groves and nature walks produces a lavish and awesome display of human creativity and imagination.

Our Master Creator who gifted these artists with skill and talent in the physical realm has no less gifted other artists who do not deal in paint, clay and stone but who reflect His love of ingenuity, originality, inspiration in their works.

I know several of the world's most inspired spiritual artists personally. They paint and sculpt not with brush or knife, but with the imagination and creativity of spirit-filled lives. Their masterpieces do not hang in renowned art galleries or auspicious museums. Audiences do not gather to gawk at their work and marvel at their talent. Their labor does not sell for thousands of dollars. These artists paint with the colors of love and encouragement. They mold with kindness. They write with joy and goodness, and the world they touch is embossed with the Creator's hand.

The works of these Masters adorn the walls of our hearts. We stand breathless with the beauty of God's handiwork through the lives of these obedient artists.

One of these Masters, Donna, designs art with encouragement and fabric. "Wrap yourself in God's love," she said, gifting me with a full-size handmade quilt. Each square holds a heart, and each heart a Bible verse, direct from the inspiration of God. *"For I am your provider, and I meet all your needs ... My plan for your future has always been filled with hope ... You are my treasured possession ... For I am your greatest encourager."* The words seep into my soul, and I am enveloped in their warmth. The quilt enfolds me. A masterpiece of encouragement, unrivaled in the art world, is added to my heart's gallery.

As bold, brash and startling as any Van Gogh, Lois splashes the colors of excitement and fun across the canvas of her daily life and the lives of those around her. Unexpectedly, she splatters a gleaming star on my canvas—tuition to a writers' conference—because, she says, "You can do this, darling! You really need to write!" And the sky is aglow with possibility, more brilliant than the original *Starry Night*.

Subdued tones, gentle colors, a Monet-like treasure of comfort and peace paints another canvas. A Thanksgiving Day toboggan accident, resulting in a broken leg, ankle, and foot, left me immobile. How would my house be maintained? How would I even get to the kitchen? God covered fears with the love of friends: Sue, Lisa, and Steve cleaned the house before I left the hospital, Trev and Casie moved a bed to the downstairs, another friend showed up faithfully once a week with a McDonald's burger, one friend brought a ceramic gingerbread house with flashing lights and music from the *Nutcracker* to delight, another brought a lovely bracelet and wishes that I would be up and about to wear it soon. Calls, cards, soup, visits. Kindness and service painted a masterpiece of love in my heart.

Friends mix through our daily journeys, like the subtle paints of the Impressionists, with phone calls, a dinner or movie invite, a pan of brownies, a birthday breakfast, a surprise gift at the backdoor. Their creativity abounds and deepens the hue and richness of their works of art. My personal collection of masterpieces is not a static representation of genius displayed in a museum. It moves and breathes with God's power and presence as He changes and molds life through the touch of those around us.

I survey again the imaginative works of spiritual sensitivity and artistry in my gallery. I stand amazed and blessed. No museum of antiquities here. Rather, a temple of friendship and goodness creatively shaped and inspired by the Great Master's hand.

Serving and helping others are God's tools of purpose for the journey. Do you feel useless? Do you lack meaning and direction? Take up the tools of the road God designed for fruit-filled living. Look for someone to encourage every day. Paint a portrait of love in someone's life with your kindness. Love is our purpose. Love is the art of our hearts.

Encouragement for Your Walk

"Therefore encourage one another and build each other up, just as in fact you are doing" (1Thessalonians 5:11). When the Walk weighs heavy and trudging the road seems intolerable, the kindness of friends encourages and enriches. Is the character of Jesus visible in your friends? Is the character of Jesus visible in you? *Be* a spiritual artist, coloring the lives of others with a touch of the divine. This is the high and holy purpose and calling of our lives.

Thank you, Lord, for the gift of friends. The Walk weaves long and rough through the years without their encouragement. Give us continual inspiration and ideas to lighten the load of others. Make us artists of love for the kingdom.

Part 5
Enjoy the Scenery

"This is winter on Layton.
A waiting, a pause, a breath-holding,
A Lazarus tomb, expectant, a resurrection
in three days.
Hope, it's coming.
New life, warmth, greens, buds, fruits.
He never fails, ever faithful, ever bringing
new from old, beauty from ashes,
life from death, growth.
The Great Maker, Renewer,
will perform the miracle
of Hope."

Jo Ann Walczak

18. Winter Magnificat

"We need to drink in beauty wherever we can get it," author John Eldridge wrote. Drink in the beauty along your road, eyes wide open to see it—though they may be blurred by tears.

Astilbe, asleep beside the drive.
Peonies, cone flowers, day lilies,
    Burrowed beneath down bits of snow,
    Energizing, strengthening for their grand appearance.
Rampant violets whose wild race about the yard is
    Temporarily stilled, silent, awaiting the next season's dance.
Pine trees, branches iced to bending, green dresses white tinged,
    Swaying at the ball that is winter.
Garden soil, resting, readying for
    The unfettered abundance of tomatoes, beans.
Forest, aglitter in splintered sun,
    Diamonds, horizon strewn.
Flakes swirl, east-west, north-south to an unheard symphony.
    Unbroken slate of white, clean, unsullied.
House, shingle-heavy, nobly faces storm
    And completes its mission—Shelter.

Encouragement for Your Walk

Hope is the message of season's change on the road we walk. The hope of spring is as certain as the hope of snow in a Pennsylvania winter. The seasons of our lives: childhood, education, marriage, child-rearing, jobs, retirement, aging—the rolling on of the seasons of our lives can foster fear, uneasiness. Anxiety trails change and whispers panic. Hope is the antidote for the flux and instability of life.

Hope, an antidote for instability. The first snow fell on Thanksgiving night. The fresh snow called for adventure. Four-year-old Wyatt clamored for the first toboggan run of the season by moonlight. Unfamiliar with the hill and the ground's topography are unimportant when the grandchildren want to ride the snow. Tucked between my legs, Wyatt and I skittered faster than I expected down the slope. I feared what might lie ahead with a little one in front, so I threw my leg off the toboggan to slow us down. We hit hard—a ditch at the bottom. My foot took the brunt of the hit. When I looked at it, my foot lay limp, off to the side, loosed from its proper place at the end of my leg.

A broken leg, broken ankle, broken foot remained. Rod, plate. Hope in change and instability. "Will I ever walk normally again?" I queried the physical therapist. "We will have to see how it heals," he responded. Hope. I hoped to walk normally again.

Put your trust in the One who never changes like the shifting of sands or the flow of seasons. The Maker and Sustainer of nature has compassion for you. His love will never fail. For the one who walks trusting Him, hope will reign because with Him hope is a certainty. When a new season of life begins and things start to change, perhaps for the worse, remember God's promise:

"Yet this I call to mind and therefore I have hope: Because of the Lord's great love we are not consumed, for his compassions never fail. They are new every morning: great is your faithfulness. I say to myself, 'The LORD is my portion, therefore I will wait for him.' The LORD is good to those whose hope is in him, to the one who seeks him" (Lamentations 3:21-25).

19. Day Lilies in Bloom

The day lilies bloomed today on Layton.

Since the first violets spread across the lawn in April and the forsythia burst into vibrant yellow, each flower in the yard has had its week or two "in the sun" on glorious display. Daffodils peeked through the cold earth, glad to have weathered the last of the frigid temperatures. Then the lily-of-the-valley crept around the backyard with their tiny white bells tinkling silently.

Three delicate pink azalea bushes proclaimed their survival through the bitter winter of the North while the lilacs popped wildly in deep purple and snowy white from overgrown trees bordering the yard. One hung heavily with flowers like a crop of ripe grapes ready for harvest. Their aroma wafted richly around the neighborhood.

No passerby could ignore the rhododendron, the "in-your-face" queen of spring blooms. Each flower the size of a small child's head, the purple-pink handfuls of loveliness dominated the yard's color scheme. Every yard seemed to boast a massive pile of rhodies.

Almost simultaneously, the pink roses joined the peonies in a glorious display. Nestled beside the peonies, testament to my poor planting judgment, the roses outdid themselves this year in size and quantity. The peonies, a last holdout from my grandmother's garden planted over fifty years ago here on Layton, boast a rare maroon shade that is nothing short of breathtaking.

The peonies are the flower I await impatiently, perhaps because they remind me of my grandmother. The Chinese adore the peony. They know and appreciate imperial and royal beauty. Many of their scroll paintings feature peonies. I bought such a scroll on a visit to China, and I enjoy the image of a peony all year. Their beauty in my yard is short-lived. They often succumb to heavy rains that cause the luxurious petals to fall limply. Even the roses paled beside the peonies.

The elephant-ear hosta leaves spread three feet in every direction, a natural tent for my grandsons' hide-and-seek games. Tall shoots, bearing white flowers, begin to climb out of the depths of the hosta to open banner-like in early July. Next to the hosta, the astilbe form a defensive front to the encroaching daisies, which cannot be contained. The gentle, pink plumes of the astilbe wave delicately, a driveway border and eye-catcher.

Summer is in full swing. The half-century old tiger lilies return for one more season, another inheritance from my grandmother's garden. The tiny buds on the tomato plants, zucchini, beans and peas look promising. August may bring a sweet harvest.

My gardens leave me in awe. Each year the cycle continues, unchanged, each flower taking the stage at the time appointed by the Creator. The cycle has never varied in my fifty years of observation. I consider the beauty, the constancy, the punctuality, the creativity and imagination in the making of a flower, and I am convinced, yet again, of the presence of the Creator and His faithfulness and dependability. The flowers display His character—filled with beauty and goodness, exemplars of supreme creativity. In my garden I stand, awed by its Maker.

And today the day lilies bloomed. They bloom, as their name obviously suggests, just for a day. In the morning dew I check the garden and there they are—faces upturned, stretching their purple and cream or purplish-rust or neon yellow arms in every direction. Their beauty screams away at the corner of my house all day, demanding attention. But when the sun sets and the cool of night draws over the yard, the day lilies curl up and shrivel away. The next morning, they are gone, replaced by the bud further down on the stem which, in its turn, now tilts its face upward and splashes its glory everywhere—for a day.

Psalm 144:4 says, *"Man is like a breath; his days are like a fleeting shadow."* The day lilies remind me that our lives, in the scheme of history, are like a breath, blooming for a day and passing quickly from the earth. Day lilies adapt to various soil and light conditions, can survive in a wide range of climates, are suitable for all landscapes, and even tolerate drought.

Do we face each day with the same resilience and strength? Like the other flowers in my yard, the day lily's loveliness is not an accident. The Master Gardener tends His garden with provision and care. The day lily wisely rests in His sovereignty, eager to bloom in the morning and to recede into glory at the end of the day. How well do we rest in God's sovereignty, ready to live today or face our end at sunset?

For our "moment in the sun," can we rest in our Maker's care? Can we trust Him to bring the sun, the rain, strength and resilience? For our moment in the sun, I pray that we can bloom like the day lily—face upturned, arms outstretched, screaming gloriously, a reflection of His beauty from our corner of the yard.

Our journeys should be walked with all senses alert, not only to the people around us, but also to the created world. No better reflection of God can be found than in the constancy, power, wisdom and imagination of God as seen in His creation. Eyes-wide. Look around and fall in love with our Creator through His handiwork. Observe.

Encouragement for Your Walk

For our "moment in the sun," may we rest in God's care, eager to bloom each morning in His sovereignty and recede into glory at the end of our journey. But what about our blooming depends on us? What must we do to bloom in beauty for our "one day"?

Jesus is clear about how we should live for our one day in the sun. He tells us not to worry about what we will eat or drink or wear, for these are the things people worry about who are not walking with the Savior. Jesus reminds us God knows we need these things, so he says to do this: *"Seek His kingdom and His righteousness and all these things will be given to you as well. Therefore, do not worry about tomorrow, for tomorrow will worry about itself. Each day has enough trouble of its own"* (Matthew 6:33-34).

Father God Creator, help us to rest in your care and provision, confident of your presence and work in us, yielded fully to the beauty you have planned for our lives. Grant us the wisdom to seek you in all things and to hunger and thirst after right living in your sight. Let our one day in the sun be a shining glory for you.

20. We Need Beauty

Florida in mid-winter jars the senses.

A trip from the Northeast to Florida in February? A jolting delight, for Florida has not tucked its growth away for a season of rest. It breathes life and color.

Florida's scenery spelled change from Layton's snowy landscape. A Florida visit rushed at me like a 3D, multi-colored, psychedelic production of light, sounds, and smells. The gray of our Pennsylvania winter faded fast in the Florida sunshine. Frankly, breathless and aghast might describe a Northerner's reaction to its teeming life, movement, and fluctuating blues and greens when our Pennsylvania senses are still frozen in January white.

Florida invites northern friends to soak up the sun's warmth, and I did, but—mostly, I saw God and His hand in and on the natural world.

God's creative presence was evidenced …

- In rooty mangrove forests consuming the beaches, providing cover and food for an array of beach critters and plants.
- In Charlotte Harbor, Sarasota Bay, and the Gulf of Mexico, glistening, shimmering, sparklng, massive, ever-dancing beneath the sun, a circumference of original life.
- In brown and white pelicans, majestic scions of the skies; ibis, skittering like chickens through the sand; great blue herons, stately, tall before the sea; snowy egrets, tropical snow against the green of mangrove and blue of sea; osprey, searching hawk-like for their next dinner; gulls, noisily littering the sky.

- In the crabs, scurrying among the mangrove and burrowing in the sand; in the dolphin, elusive divers on the horizon.
- In the hibiscus, flashing their giant red, yellow, and orange faces about the landscape; in the royal palm, stately, erect at their hundred-foot vantage.
- In shells, like our northern snowflakes, each an individual with its own characteristics: whelks, conch, augur, cockles, pens, barnacles, a plethora of form, shape, texture.

Florida in February is a tribute to the imagination, creativity, and beauty of God. Each of His creations, existing to the beauty God placed within it.

John Eldridge wrote in his book, *Waking the Dead*, "We need beauty; that's clear enough from the fact that God has filled the world with it…We need to drink in beauty wherever we can get it…These are all gifts to us from God's generous heart."

Scenery along our Walks might change daily: sunshine and tropical colors one day, problems and chaos the next. Walking with godly consistency, when everything around us is in flux and change, like the weather, pushes the envelope of our stability. This is yet another reason to lean into the One who never changes, who is the same yesterday, today, and forever, and who calls us to live in this world of change grounded in His principles for living.

The imagination, creativity, and beauty displayed in God's creations are intrinsic to them. They do not struggle to live beautifully. They do not drive to achieve that beauty. They simply *are* beautiful because God made them that way, and everything God makes is good (1 Timothy 4:4).

"I see beauty in YOU, too," He whispers. "I made you and I saved you from the self-will that has soiled your living. I live through Christ, My Son, in you. Live to that beauty." The sea, the pelicans, the whelk, the palm, and the dolphin live to the beauty they've been given. "Live to the beauty you are," God reminds us.

Live to Christ in us. Be what He made us to be—Beauty.

Encouragement for Your Walk

Each day as your Walk begins, remind yourself, "I am a chosen, treasured possession of the God of the universe." Walk worthy of that calling. Live to Christ inside you. Be what He made you to be—a beautiful reflection of Him. Chin up. Eyes to the sky. You belong to the King. Beautiful.

Yes, Florida epitomizes beauty, but there is something about Layton Road, the ordinary place we walk, too, a beauty unlike the Sunshine State but glorious, nonetheless. Wherever we walk, when we walk with God, there should be an aura of His presence. Iceland, Kenya, Mongolia, Tasmania, see God in our changing surroundings. Be assured He is there.

Creator God, help us to walk in your ways, doing those things in which you delight. Help us to live worthy of our Maker so you are seen in us. Thank you for calling us your chosen and treasured children.

21. Vine and Branches

We spent the Ides of March off Layton because the sap was running and we wanted to follow the flow. Evidently, sap runs when the nights are cold and the days are warm.

I took my grandsons to a maple sugar farm. The experience was much less harrowing than our snowshoe escapade at the state park. In fact, today's adventure involved food—a perk that always makes a grandma-adventure fun.

We trekked to Burke's Maple Farm deep in the farm country of Lackawanna County for their open house weekend. Mr. Burke and his mother walked us through the maple syrup-making process.

I envisioned a maple sugar farm with little wooden spigots drilled in the sides of maples with a bucket dangling below each spigot. But we had stepped out of that Norman Rockwell painting and into the twenty-first century. This farm boasted all the equipment of a state-of-the-art maple sugaring powerhouse. In fact, the farm looked almost like a scene from a sci-fi thriller.

Thousands of maples, four football field spaces in every direction, linked to each other with miles and miles of plastic tubing—plastic tubing up the mountainside, plastic tubing down the hill, plastic tubing across the meadows, plastic tubing weaving serpentine through the forest as far as the eye could see, forming a maze of interconnected, living, breathing, sugar-producing trees.

I wondered if the deer stumbled through this plastic labyrinth, entwining their antlers in plastic tubing, or if the black bears pulled the tubing apart to sit beneath the maples, sucking the liquid candy until they lapsed into a sugar coma.

But it is vacuum cylinders that suction the sap through the tubing, and the sap runs, throbbing and shushing across the woodlands, like the circulatory system of a giant, towards the heart of the farm, the boiler. The tubing rises above our heads, over the road, and dumps into the gleaming, stainless-steel collector—the life blood of nature, bringing healthy sweetness to greenhorns like us.

Amazing.

A full-time contractor, Mr. Burke runs the maple sugaring operation as a hobby—granted, an expansive one—that must involve spending a lot of time with plastic tubing and Mrs. Burke's homemade maple muffins, maple cookies, and maple candy. She appears to be a chef extraordinaire with all things maple.

There were samples, of course, so the boys headed for the muffins and cookies. The maple glazed walnuts scored with all of us. We bought two packages, finishing most of them off on the ride home. Of course, we bought a king's ransom of syrup for pancakes, too. The plan is to make the walnuts this week with our fresh syrup so the glory of March will last a bit longer.

We already have a grandma-adventure planned for the Ides of March next year. It will have something to do with plastic tubing and maple glazed walnuts.

The interconnected tubing, extending for acres and carrying the maples' sugary lifeblood, reminded me of the twisted, interconnected metaphorical miles of vines, linking believers to Jesus Christ. Even in the spiritual realm, it's all about connection to the power source. John 15:4-8 warns us to stay connected:

"Remain in me, as I also remain in you. No branch can bear fruit by itself; it must remain in the vine. Neither can you bear fruit unless you remain in me. I am the vine; you are the branches. If you remain in me and I in you, you will bear much fruit; apart from me you can do nothing. If you do not remain in me, you are like a branch that is thrown away and withers; such branches are picked up, thrown into the fire and burned. If you remain in me and my words remain in you, ask whatever you wish, and it will be done for you. This is to my Father's glory, that you bear much fruit, showing yourselves to be my disciples" (John 15:4-8).

Our connection to Jesus, like a vine, is the only way we can bear the fruits of love, joy, peace, patience, kindness, goodness, faithfulness, and self-control. Take away our connection to Jesus, and the fruit shrivels up and dies. God wants us to be fruitful, and the lifeblood, pouring to and through us from our Redeemer, produces the power needed. A day at the maple sugar farm provided a picture of God's plan for staying connected to Jesus for the power to bear fruit.

Encouragement for Your Walk

Reading God's Word daily, spending time talking to Him, getting together with others who love Jesus, going to a church where Christ is honored—these are the ways our souls stay connected to our source. Jesus called it abiding, allowing His personhood and fruit to flow through us like the living life blood of the maples flows its sweetness to the world. These disciplines of the Christian Walk will bear fruit in our lives and overflow to others. Do you want to see more kindness, gentleness, self-control, and love in your life? Hook up to God through the "tubing" of spiritual connectedness and watch the fruit bloom.

And use a field trip to a maple sugar farm to teach the children this lesson for living well.

Father God, help us to stay connected to Jesus, abiding in Him through time in your Word and time at your feet. Help the fruit of our lives to grow abundantly.

22. Rest Awhile

The relentless routine of life on our roads has made vacationing an American ritual. Schools and businesses comply with a person's need to step off the road and out of the hectic pace of life to rest.

But America didn't invent the idea of rest. Rest is God-ordained. He rested after six days of creation. He told us to rest after six days of work. Rest is written into our manual of life on the road. Rest means not working, not following the daily routines of labor.

Americans often equate rest with vacations rather than with time spent in God's presence, drinking in His glory and finding refreshment for the next leg of the journey on Monday morning.

But some vacations can completely reorient our minds to God's power and creativity in nature. To me, camping satisfies that goal. Sitting, sleeping, and walking in the great outdoors among some of God's most finely formed creations is the equivalent of experiencing God close-up and personal among the beauties He has fashioned. Drink it in and rest with Him.

Experience has taught our family the joys and values of camping for reorienting our minds, promoting family talk-time and togetherness, and for appreciating the glory of God through the world His hands have touched and formed.

In the early sixties Dad launched my decades-long camping career. I was twelve, so, initially, camping seemed like more work than necessary. I was annoyed with carrying water to cook, chagrined with heating water to wash, and further annoyed with five of us in sleeping bags, jammed shoulder-to-shoulder and butt-to-butt in our umbrella tent. Perhaps it is in just such circumstances that children learn flexibility and gratefulness whatever the situation. Certainly, learning to live and work like a pioneer is character-building.

Our maiden adventure was to the Great Smoky Mountains National Park. Signs for safety with bears were everywhere. Dad slept with an ax, locked the food in our car, and lay expectantly all night while bears snuffled around the campsite. That was camping trip number one.

Even with all the inconveniences, I realized as a young teen, camping was a way to see the world on a shoestring and have some wonderful adventures besides. Seeing the grander heavenly scope of camping took a bit longer.

"Shoestring" vacations were the operative words when, as a single mom of a four and six-year-old, I realized that, if I was ever going to give my boys some adventure, show them our country, and have conversation opportunities totally about God's incredible creative power, it would have to be in a tent.

A two-man pup tent was big enough and cheap enough. Peanut butter sandwiches made menus easy for breakfast, lunch, and dinner, and off we went each summer for the next ten years. In those days, we could camp for under ten dollars a night at a walk-in site. We camped in most national parks and visited countless points-of-interest between Northeast Pennsylvania and Little River, South Carolina, where we collapsed at Pa and MaMa's home.

Chincoteague and Assateague, Williamsburg, the Blue Ridge Mountains, the Cherokee Indian Reservation, the Outer Banks, the Smokies and more . . . horses, bears, snakes, Indians, the ocean. This was living adventure for a single mom and her boys. This was helping them to see a Father God who designed the world beautifully and would do the same thing for the boys He loved, with their cooperation.

The official and formal end to years of family camping came when the boys were fourteen and sixteen. Summer jobs loomed for the college bound, so a final, big bash campout was planned. Pa and MaMa were included. I purchased an old conversion van in the Paper Shop, a local listing of used items for sale. The van, already clocked at ninety thousand miles, needed tires, and lacked air conditioning which became an issue in Death Valley. We replaced the tires, but the air conditioning remained airless. Undeterred, the five of us set off across the United States in pursuit of as many national parks as we could find.

The trip would cover over ten thousand miles in our fifty days on the road, and it would take us from East coast to West coast, from Mexico to Canada. The southern route took us west with stops in Nashville, Hot Springs, Arkansas, Dallas, Juarez, Mexico, Death Valley and on to the Pacific. We followed the Pacific coast into British Columbia and Alberta, south into Montana, and with a final swing across the northern states. For part of the trip, we followed the old Lee and Lincoln Highways across America.

The van had a pull-out bed in the back which we reserved for Pa and MaMa during the entire trip. The boys and I slept in our tent, a four-man dome—easy up, easy down. Sometimes we froze at night, like when we camped near the base of the glacier at Lake Louise in British Columbia and awoke each morn exhaling frost from a breathing hole in our sleeping bags. Sometimes we baked, like in the high desert near Tucson, Arizona, where the temps hovered at 105 degrees.

Daily, we made memories: the "Going to the Sun" highway in Glacier National Park, Montana; a solitary walk through the Muir Woods among the giant sequoias in northern California; a drive through Death Valley in the Southwest with the windows up (in our non-air-conditioned van because MaMa had some crazy theory about keeping it cool inside); exploring the food stands in Juarez, Mexico; and walking, always walking, the trails in Yellowstone, the Sierras, Yosemite, and the Grand Canyon. This was the adventure of a lifetime, a forever family memory, an epic journey, a walk among God's most spectacular creations.

The result: the family was still talking to each other after fifty days of camping, and I prayed God had become a reality for them. Both of my sons have made camping a major activity for their own families. Parenting three children each, Bryan and Trevor have graduated from the tents of their youth to RVs. They still love finding beautiful places in America to camp, and the joys of sitting around campfires at night have never been lost. We are into our fourth generation of family campers.

THE WALK ON LAYTON

Thirty years later, the boys continue to mention the significance of that trip in their lives.

Our "rest" experience with God took us to almost every one of America's national parks in the lower forty-eight states and to countless national monuments, a total of about forty-three altogether.

Ken Burns wrote, "Our national parks are America's best idea." Truly. And they are also America's way to point us to God, for the Creator's fingerprints are evident everywhere in nature's beauty and glory. Creation was God's best idea.

Horace Albright, one of the founders of the National Park System, said, "The parks are something more enduring than we are. They were designed by God..."

Our lives are brief, but in the great outdoors we see continuity. Stand on a glacier, under a giant Sequoia, or on a Grand Canyon overlook. Problems dwarf in the face of God's majesty and power. Hot springs and geysers bubbling from deep in the earth, Mount St. Helen's witness to the inner power, towering pines in rain forests of the Northwest—all display an awe-inspiring majesty no man could manufacture.

These wonders take us out of our circumstances and self-absorption. We see ourselves as we really are—a small part of God's limitless and magnificent creation. Scripture attests to God's hand in it all: *"For since the creation of the world God's invisible qualities—His eternal power and divine nature—have been clearly seen, being understood from what has been made, so that people are without excuse"* (Romans 1:20, *The Message*).

On the arch above the northern entrance to Yellowstone, the purpose of the park system is stated: "For the benefit and enjoyment of the people." Enjoyment, inspiration, a God-encounter—the vacation of a lifetime awaits.

I'm reminded of a World War II song my dad often sang on the road: "Pack up your troubles in an old kit bag and smile, smile, smile!" Pandemics, wars, terrorists, whatever the state of the world, we can continue to gather our camping gear and kit bags and plan a restful time in God's tabernacle of the outdoors. Get ready to smile, smile, smile.

You can too. America is unique, inspirational, and breathtaking beyond imagination, a welcome and crucial reminder of who and what we are.

> Walking on Layton
> but encouraging you to
> go camping,
> see America and
> Rest.

Encouragement for Your Walk

"Let the heavens rejoice, let the earth be glad; let the sea resound, and all that is in it, Let the fields be jubilant, and everything in them; let all the trees of the forest sing for joy. Let all creation rejoice before the Lord ..." (Psalm 96:11-13). God's creation rejoices and sings of His power in its beauty and awesomeness.

Lord, as we walk our roads, help us pause to appreciate your magnificence and splendor in the world around us. And sometimes, encourage us to get off the routine of our roads and walk, awed and blessed, through your Creation. Thank you for rest.

Part 6
Friends and Family

"Do not waste time bothering whether you 'love' your neighbor; act as if you did. As soon as we do this, we find one of the great secrets. When you are behaving as if you loved someone, you will presently come to love him."

C. S. Lewis
British Author

23. Dining Table Relationships

November. The culinary extravaganza of the holidays begins. Food menus are planned, and the shopping and cooking tasks explode. My sons' favorite menus contain kielbasa and pierogi from the traditions of their Polish grandmother, our well-established Christmas brunch of quiche and crepes, Dad's Welsh cookies, and my sister's cherry-rolled, German pastry stollen. And all of it will be piled on and enjoyed at our dining room table.

My grandmother's table is the focal point of our feeding frenzy. The table dominates our dining room as it has for the past ninety years. Except during a few difficult years when the dining room converted into a hospital room, and the table took up residence elsewhere in the house, the drop-leaf mahogany with claw feet has seated five generations of our family.

Every life event for all our generations has centered around the old drop-leaf. Last Thanksgiving twenty of us squeezed around the table with the aid of an additional collapsible length. Now, shaky and unstable, I sometimes wonder how long we can continue to re-screw and re-bolster before our dining room table goes the way of our older generations.

One year a professional carpenter came the week before Thanksgiving to hammer it back into shape. One-by-one, the rickety chairs gave out, sometimes with a relative or friend on them. A few new chairs surround the table. Our dining table boasts a lengthy, hardy life.

Hospitality has been practiced here. Distant relatives, children's birthday parties, neighbors, school chums, church friends, book club, new acquaintances, committees—a parade of hundreds have pulled up a chair to the drop-leaf through the years. My excitement always peaks as I dig out Nana's china, find an appropriate centerpiece, and iron Mom's embroidered napkins, for I am anticipating the joy of sharing food and my table with others. No mission field has been more fertile.

In ancient cultures, the meal was a setting for blessing, too. Around a meal elder members of the family would pass on approval, guidance, and wisdom. Time together meant connection and intimacy among family members and their guests, a private sharing of lives. And this is what Nana's mahogany drop-leaf has become for us through the years—a haven for deeper relationships, family stability, and love. Our table is a place to feed our spirits with God's best even when we may be fed up with life.

The Bible says it is the desire of Jesus to dine with us. He seeks intimacy and connection with us over the table of our daily lives. He listens to us and He wants to know, "So tell me about your day?" I'd like to think he'd say at the table. "What made you happy? What challenges did you face? What is heavy on your heart?" Of course, Jesus knows the answers to these questions, but He wants us to talk to Him. He wants us to pour out our concerns, joys, and failures. He wants us to pull up our rickety chairs close to Him, relax, and talk. He seeks a dinner table-kind of relationship with us.

Scripture continually affirms Jesus' desire to sit and sup with those He loves. After all, His first miracle was performed at a wedding feast with friends and family. Consider the night before His death when the last and most beautiful fellowship He wanted with His friends was around a table where He enacted the brokenness and givenness of His life for them. And then, of course, there is the promise of heaven and a wedding feast with Jesus and us, His church. The finest moments of life and eternity take place around a table.

In Jesus' time meals were designed for relationship building. Lying down to eat was a common tradition granted to free men. Free men could relax and enjoy hours of visiting and eating. A slave would not have such luxury. Dinners might go on for hours as course after course was served.

Eastern cultures always serve meals in stages, allowing guests to relish and enjoy one food before the next comes from the kitchen. In China it was not uncommon for a meal to have eight courses: soup, several kinds of fish, rice, noodles, duck, pork, dumplings, and fruit. As in most Eastern cultures, the Chinese designed their meals for conversation and relationships. Guests sat at the table for several hours, with plenty of time to talk about countless aspects of their lives. When Jesus invites us to dine with Him, His intention is to enjoy our company, be with us, and share our hearts.

A guest list suggested by Jesus in Scripture would not include the noblemen, wealthy businessmen, or leaders in the church or government. In a Luke 14:12-14 parable Jesus describes the guest list: *"When you give a luncheon or dinner, do not invite your friends, your brothers or sisters, your relatives or your rich neighbors; if you do, they may invite you back and so you will be repaid. But when you give a banquet, invite the poor, the crippled, the lame, the blind, and you will be blessed. Although they cannot repay you, you will be repaid at the resurrection of the righteous."* This godly standard for hospitality would be counter-cultural in the 21st century. A true and committed Walk with Jesus will usually rub the hackles of the cultural norm.

A wedding feast? A last supper? Why would Jesus, God's Son, seek intimacy with dinner companions whom the critics of His day considered less than desirable? Love is the only answer—His unwavering desire to bring a divine, faithful abiding love to the table of our lives.

I am reminded of my kitchen table in China. The table was a perfect four-square. I thought the drawers on each side were a nice addition, a place to keep vitamins, silverware, papers. But one day a visitor at my table revealed something unexpected. He lifted the top of the table off and flipped it over, revealing a complete mahjong board. The drawers were for each player's tiles. God knows our hidden sins and problems, hidden away in the secret drawers of our lives, yet He still chooses to eat at the mahjong tables and mahogany drop-leaves of our lives with us. Such love.

Ask Jesus to sit at your table daily. Then invite Him to take a Walk with you.

Encouragement for Your Walk

"Here I am! I stand at the door and knock. If anyone hears my voice and opens the door, I will come in and eat with that person and they with me" (Revelation 3:20). Have you invited Jesus to come into your life, to walk, work, and dine with you? To be present in the dailiness of your life as a friend and to relish the intimacy of His company?

If you have, then the next step is to practice Biblical hospitality. Give others what God has given you—hospitality. Hospitality involves all aspects of serving others, not just cooking and serving meals, but demonstrating love, care, and concern in any way that helps others and honors God. Giving someone a ride to a doctor appointment, playing with a neighbor child who is missing a parent in the home, delivering a bag of groceries to someone in need are ways to serve others, demonstrate hospitality, and show respect to God. On the journey, check to see who is walking beside you in need of assistance. Offer help and pull up a chair at the table of their lives.

24. Making Memories

It's Memorial Day weekend, and I'm enjoying the view on Layton.

The lawn, thick and green with last night's rain, awaits my Toro. Several mowers can be heard up and down our road. Families of wrens, robins, and chickadees have called the Justus Symphony Orchestra to concert in the old oak, whose arms have draped over the yard for a hundred years. The cat lies lazily in the shade of the picnic table, swatting listlessly at low-flying bugs. The cukes, tomatoes, and beans peek through the soil of my small raised-bed garden. The Adirondack chairs under the sprawling maple in the rear of the yard sit like thrones, presiding regally over this small world.

It could be Memorial Day, 1957. The view from my porch hasn't changed much in the past fifty years.

Fifty years ago, this already-old house buzzed with picnic preparations. Memorial Day launched the summer season when the city cousins from North Scranton trekked "up the country." The extended family came every weekend in the summer for all-day backyard cookouts, to escape the city heat, and to "kibbitz" with the family.

In those days this house belonged to my grandmother, Nana Evans, known as Aunt Ethel to the cousins. My mom, dad, sisters, and I lived in the house next door to Nana. Our two yards converged with plenty of room for children to grow up.

Summer preparations began in earnest for this first picnic of the season. Dad washed off the metal glider, pulled out the aluminum yard chairs and rethreaded their frayed nylon seats. He hammered the badminton net into place, rehung the tether ball, and filled the grill with charcoal. "Annie, where's the...?" Dad called intermittently to my mother in the kitchen. "Annie," a whirling dervish in her own right, swept about the kitchen preparing her favorite Jello mold recipe and macaroni salad.

The coming of the cousins brewed high excitement.

Nana and her sisters, Aunt Peggy, Aunt Ruthie, and Aunt Millie, reigned as matriarchs of the brood. Aunt Ruthie lived in Chinchilla. Aunt Peggy lived on Margaret Avenue in Scranton near her daughter Peg, and her son Bill lived just a street over on Edna Avenue. Aunt Peggy's other son Bob and his wife Mickey had moved after World War II to that haven for post-war vets, Levittown, in search of a job that didn't involve the coal mines.

All of the men of those two generations had put in some time in the local coal mines: Grandpa Evans spent most of his working life in the mines; Uncle Gordy, Aunt Peggy's husband, Aunt Ruthie's husband Uncle Victor, and Aunt Millie's husband Uncle Cliff had their hands to the pick and shovel until the demise of the industry. Even my dad earned his first paychecks from the Olyphant breaker. Summer afternoons in the country gave them a chance to blow off the soot and breathe fresh air.

Aunt Ruthie didn't have any children, but Aunt Peggy's children and grandchildren made it a party. We had cousins in every age group from Peg's three girls, Lynn, Beth, and Lori, to Bill's children, Glenny, Phil, and Les. Sometimes cousins Bob and Mickey came up from Levittown. When Bob's family came, the excitement and activity increased with his twin sons Bob and Bill and daughters, Joan and Gail. Our cup overflowed with cousins and a bevy of adults to supervise. Everyone had a buddy.

The ghosts of memories dance around the yard this Memorial Day: I see Phil hiding behind the front hedges in our twilight hide-and-seek game. The twins clank the lids on their jars as they corral lightning bugs. "Hey, Joey. Can you hit this?" Sid yells to my dad as he slams the birdie over the badminton net and into the lilac bush.

Nana and her sisters laugh and talk simultaneously at high volume under the shade of the apple tree. Mom runs in and out of the kitchen with tablecloths and food. "Annie, don't forget the ketchup. The dogs are ready!" Dad announces to the yard in general as Jiggsy, our beagle, runs between legs, seeking what he might devour.

One year Glenny ripped open her leg on the chicken wire around my dad's new seedlings. The pitch of the old aunts' cackling went up a decibel as Glenny was rushed off to the emergency room for stitches.

Another year Sid won our hearts when he took the kids horseback riding up Layton at Bill Jones's riding stable.

Gail, Glenny, and I would swing on the front porch glider, sharing secrets about our parents and boys.

If there weren't enough paper plates, my mother, never a slave to fashion, was known to rip them and serve the kids on half plates.

Bill's wife, Miar, always managed to bring the winning covered dish delight. A bit more *avant-garde* than the rest, she actually searched out recipes and bedazzled our taste buds.

At the end of the picnic day, our family stood around the yard saying good-byes, planning next week's picnic, hugging, and waving the cousins off to their distant homes in Scranton, twelve miles away. A satisfied sense of belonging and continuity tucked me into bed although I doubt if I could have identified the reason for my joy at that time.

Today the yard is silent except for the clatter and spontaneity of my memories. Nana and the aunts, Peggy and Sid, Bill and Miar, Bob and Mickey, and Mom and Dad are all gone. I only see the cousins now at funerals. When we see each other at these *last* goodbyes, it's evident that the cousin bond was deeply forged in our childhoods. One of the twins, Bob, reminded me at a recent funeral, "My best childhood memories were in your yard."

The cousins scattered to the wind when we began the migration to college. Most never returned to Scranton. Lynn married a Dutchman and moved to the Netherlands; Phil had a successful career with the FBI and then retired to Memphis; Les, an in-demand orthopedic surgeon in Kansas City, continues to practice there; the twins, best friend-brothers, lived in Bucks County and juggled several enterprises until Bill's recent passing; Gail had a knitting business for a while in Pittsburgh, and

Glenny suffered as the collective recipient of the family's legendary struggle with diabetes. Most of us are grandparents now; all of us are senior citizens.

Still, I enjoy the view from my porch. The apple tree succumbed to lack of care. When it produced only quarter-sized apples, it met dad's axe. The front porch glider has seen countless coats of paint, but it stands immovable, its steel frame too heavy to lift. The other day my grandson and I tried to find the tether ball pipe, implanted somewhere mid-yard, hoping to put it back in action, but it had sunk into oblivion. The chicken wire is gone as are the aluminum chairs, but they did have a long run through three generations, thanks to my ever-mending, ever-recycling father. A modern propane grill eventually replaced the old red charcoal burner.

We still enjoy badminton, though a series of nets have been short-lived. Only Dad survived our parents' and grandparents' generations. In an attempt to maintain the badminton tradition, we modified the game so Dad, at ninety-five, could play badminton with us. Everyone on the badminton court sat in a yard chair at their assigned position to allow him the fun of playing without the effort of running around. Of course, reaching too far with the racket resulted in toppled chairs and plenty of hoots and hollering, but—Dad got to play, and we all have a cherished memory of a crazy fun afternoon of badminton that would be his last.

This Memorial Day, the yard is silent. The echoes of memories resound from oak to maple. But I continue to enjoy the view and the memories from my porch on Layton.

God's faithfulness and blessings resonate through the decades. Deaths, divorces, illness, and trouble have been as prevalent here as anywhere, but the song of our hearts should be gratefulness for God's constant love, His promise to always walk the roads of our lives with us, and to never leave us or forsake us as the years march on, even in the face of miseries common to all. A banner of God's protection and strength waves immutably before us on the Walk. We do not journey alone, and if our eyes and ears are open, God's presence stands obvious and faithful, today and every day, on Layton or wherever you live.

Encouragement for Your Walk

"Remember the days of old; consider the generations long past. Ask your father and he will tell you, your elders, and they will explain to you" (Deuteronomy 32:7 ESV).

Remember, remember, remember. The word "remember" occurs in the Bible over three hundred times. A simple command with a wealth of divine intent. God ordained the importance of memories and the significance of gratefulness for what those memories represent. Remember the events and people who have been part of your Walk. And remember to thank God for His faithfulness through generations.

Father, you have blessed us with sweet memories. Thank you, Lord, for the people you have given us along the road and for how we have learned and grown through their involvement in our lives. Give us the creativity and motivation to be memory-makers for our people. Help us to establish traditions that draw attention to you and honor you, traditions to be passed to the next generation. Thank you for your faithfulness.

25. Campfire Stories

Every Walk sees its share of unforgettable milestone events and memories worth passing down through generations as legendary stories. Of course, Jesus had the attention of His disciples—and He gets ours because He loved to tell stories of the kingdom—through parables, metaphorical stories.

Ted Talk Coach Geoffrey Berwind is quoted in *Forbes Magazine* in an article on the power of storytelling as saying, "as long as there have been campfires, humans have gathered around them and conveyed their view of the world through the use of stories. Stories are a 'shared experience'…We are hard-wired to receive information primarily through storytelling."

One of my favorite stories growing up and worthy of a campfire scare, involved Nana Jones's eightieth birthday.

Nana Jones, my dad's mother, entered the world with the turn of the twentieth century, 1900, in Liverpool, England. Recalling her age was never difficult as she rolled on in age *with* the year. So, in 1980 I determined to give her a "girl" party for her eightieth birthday, a party with her best friends.

Nana (Winnie) Jones also lived on Layton about a quarter mile up the road. Almost all of her lady friends had spent their lives on this half mile of country road between the Mt. Bethel Baptist Church, where they attended, and Justus Corners. They raised their children and grandchildren together, they ran Old Home Day every year at Mt. Bethel, they crocheted granny block afghans, knitted sweaters, hats and mittens,

THE WALK ON LAYTON

cooked up a whirlwind for covered dish dinners, worked with the Ladies Auxiliary of the Justus Fire Company, and enjoyed visiting back and forth to rock on the front porch glider and finish off a pot of tea.

I knew all of Nana Jones' friends well. We lived in the extended family of a country village and attended the same church. Our lives intersected at every point.

Florence James was Nana Jones's best friend. Florence lived just two houses away from my grandmother. Short and petitely built, Florence was the antithesis of my grandmother's tall, strongly-built physique. I can't ever remember Winnie and Florence wearing anything except house dresses, always lightly flowered and neat, even when weeding their gardens.

Betty Priest lived in the house right next to my grandmother, their back doors separated by no more than twenty yards. Mrs. Priest came over my grandmother's almost every day for tea. Nana Jones never lost her British affection for tea with milk and a few biscuits. As a child I was fascinated by her skill of reading the tea leaves left in the cup. Good friends until Betty died, leaving a gap in my grandmother's daily life, they never called each other anything except Mrs. Priest and Mrs. Jones.

The Von Storch family, the premier farming family in Justus, lived just around the corner, and Minerva, the family's matriarch, had raised a bevy of boys who romped the countryside with my dad and the Evans and Lewis boys. She knew how to handle rowdy teens and how to make the best pies in Justus. At a church dinner we vied for Mrs. Von Storch's pies.

Mildred Baker lived on Layton but further up the big hill, and Beatrice White, of the legendary White clan who originally settled the Clarks Summit area, lived over on Fairview. The women were united by age, family, church, the fire company, the Depression and the War. They survived as friends.

Florence, Betty, Minerva, Mildred and Beatrice (although I would never have considered calling them anything but "Mrs.—") composed my guest list of best friends for Nana Jones's 80th birthday party, a Who's Who of 20th Century Mothers in Justus.

Held in my front parlor, an appropriate synonym for my living room, the party featured chicken salad sandwiches and several rounds of BINGO, but it was the conversation that intrigued me.

As the ladies arrived and sat around the parlor, they began to tell their favorite story about the house. "I haven't been here since Ethel died ... Oh, it was long before that since I've been here ... We used to come often to play cards ... I'll never forget the night of the funeral ..."

I'd heard the story before from my mother and grandmother, but here sat the mothers of the neighborhood recalling an event in 1950 that left an indelible community impression—a funeral gone awry.

"It was one of the worst storms we ever had the night Bill was laid out here. Rain came in buckets. The roof nearly collapsed ... Water poured into this room ... The men had to get up on the roof in the rain and patch it up fast ... The casket sat right over there." Minerva pointed to the end of the parlor where I had lunch laid out. All eyes turned to that part of the room, and I envisioned my grandfather laid out there in his coffin.

And the recollections continued of my Grandfather Evans' funeral. Grandpa Evans constructed this house on Layton. When he died suddenly of a heart attack on the cellar steps of the house he had built and loved, his body was prepared for "viewing" and "laid out" here in the front room, probably very close to where I'm sitting now. The traditional custom of the day had people "viewed" in their own homes, rather than at a funeral home. A disconcerting thought, as the rest of the family lay upstairs in bed. It's not a custom that has carried into the 21st century. Thankfully.

The night of the "viewing," a storm hit that blew off the shingles, ripped up part of the roof, and brought gallons of water gushing down the walls to the parlor, and . . . into my grandfather's casket. The women cackled and screamed. The men of the family and the neighborhood rushed into action through pelting rain and wind, climbing to the roof and re-boarding and covering the holes. I didn't ask how they dealt with damage and drainage to the coffin and . . . Grandpa Evans.

The guests at Nana Jones's birthday party had attended the "viewing" here in my parlor in 1950, and they relished every detail of the retelling. Thirty years after the event, and it still made a great story for the neighborhood.

The Israelites experienced their share of death experiences on their long wilderness trek, stories reiterated to us in God's Word. Many of those momentous occasions were designed to be pointed reminders of His love and faithfulness. Passover, Yom Kippur, Pentecost, and several feast days celebrated important events in their history, honored and passed on traditions and stories, and helped them to understand their connection with God. Key events at these occasions would be telling the stories that originated the holiday event. Stories passed on God's legacy and reminded them of Him. God loves momentous occasions and the stories that commemorate His relationship with them.

Momentous occasions scatter the roads we walk: Thanksgiving, birthdays—death days, the circle of life here on Layton. Every special milestone, whether joy-filled or sad, marks out the passing of time and God's reoccurring faithfulness. Remember those special family stories and pass them along to your generations. Write them down. Our family will never forget grandpa's funeral story. Our stories are signposts along the road to remind us of the relentless nature of time and the devoted love of God.

Encouragement for Your Walk

The most momentous of our milestone events will be the day we glimpse the end of this difficult Walk and the gates of heaven open for us. *"Know therefore that the LORD your God is God; he is the faithful God, keeping his covenant of love to a thousand generations of those who love him and keep his commandment"* (Deuteronomy 7:9). And His covenant with us is certain: because of Jesus' sacrifice and our acceptance of Him, we will indeed have a glorious milestone resurrection in glory with Him. Tell this family story to your children and your grandchildren. Pass it on.

Father, keep us faithful to passing on the story of your covenant promises and love for us to our generations. Strengthen us to walk more closely with you each day so the comfort and companionship of Your presence on this road will explode into the joy of sitting with you in glory, face-to-face.

26. Clothes for the Road

"What should we do with the clothes?"

"I won't wear them," my sister Nancy assured us.

"Let's make a pile for Salvation Army," Sally decided.

"I'm probably the closest in size to Mom, but I'll pass," I concurred.

My mother's clothes covered the top of her bed and spilled to the floor as my sisters and I examined each piece. We fingered the blouses, slips, scarves, and pajamas and remembered: the suit she wore for the family Christmas photo, the silky nightgown that helped her to slide and turn more easily in her sleep, the pink jacket and dress I made for her first and only cruise. Each fabric and color evoked a memory. None of us relished the thought of delving into and dispersing this ocean of clothing. Perhaps we evaluated her wardrobe too soon after her death. Nothing looked good without her in it.

Our eyes roamed over some t-shirts—a white one from Mom's church, Bible Fellowship Baptist; another from Windjammer Village, her retirement homesite; a hot pink number from the Calabash mini-golf where she earned occasional pocket money. These shirts composed Mom's much-loved, relaxed, daily attire. Never a slave to fashion, mom opted for comfort.

Her Sunday clothes, many of which were hand-me-downs from one aunt or another, lay limp and lifeless despite their colorful, frilly appearance beside the t-shirts. Without the *faux* diamond pin and glitzy bracelet inherited from her mother who chose flash over comfort, or her numerous strands of beads, Mom's dress-up clothes lacked luster—even though we knew her true luster lay in her powerful personality and character. The down-home touch of glamor she saved for church and special occasions transformed her everyday t-shirt appearance. Now, all of her clothes gave up a ghost of earlier joys.

Mom's slacks, with elasticized waists to suit her growing middle girth, didn't meet our blue jean requirements. Besides, we would never admit to our need for elasticized waists.

The bed pile loomed: Mom's clothes ... Mom. The clothing and adornments of a life well-lived. The last physical shred of our connection with her. The fabrics held her smell, her hair, her presence. Shipping them off to the Salvation Army seemed brutal. And yet, what would we do with them?

Nothing in the pile moved us to say, "I want the blue blouse!" ... "I'd love to wear those khakis." ... "Oh, the red mid-calf is just my style!" ... "Now there's a coat I have to have." Truthfully, my sisters and I would probably never wear any of it.

For a while, we would bury Mom's clothes in plastic bags under the bed, like our grief, until we could face the final good-bye of pushing them down the drop box chute in the parking lot of the Salvation Army.

Eventually, even Dad grew tired of the plastic bags of clothing under the bed. They hampered the vacuum, he said, and flowed out like an obstacle course on his bedroom floor. Healing had begun. We had reached a critical decision point, a point of final separation from Mom's physical presence. The clothes had to go.

One last time, I sorted through them. Which pieces of clothing could I live without ever seeing again? Which would be a reminder of Mom, even if I never wore them? My heap of things to save began to grow. I would cut the logos off her t-shirts and put them together in some kind of display. Perhaps a quilt? Knowing my penchant for procrastination, a quilt might never materialize, but at least I would have those bits of her t-shirts. You never know.

I could wear Mom's lamb's wool coat in the dead of winter, and I wouldn't look dated. I'd look—vintage, like my friend Leslee who always wore vintage, defining her persona. Yes, I could wear some of Mom.

Among her sweaters, a gray, oversized blazer-type cardigan with wooden buttons and a collar said my name. Mom wore it daily. Its age made me wonder if she might have inherited it from Great-aunt Sarah who bought quality clothing, clothing that would have lasted these thirty years. I knew Mom hadn't bought the sweater. It was too fine a piece for her frugal wallet. The sweater stood the test of time without a hole, run, or pull to hamper its appearance. Mom had used it as her going-out, around-the-house, all-purpose garment. Even multiple washings wouldn't shake the presence of Mom from the fiber. This was the piece of Mom's clothing I wanted.

Today, the old gray sweater has become a basic part of my household wardrobe. I don it each morning for coffee as its warmth and comfort suit me better than a bathrobe. I wear it when I'm sick, enjoying the nearness of Mom as if she were nursing me back to health. I wear it to cozy up on cold winter days. Mom never moves far from my heart. In fact, her love wraps and envelops me like an old gray sweater.

When I wear the old gray, she is there. The essence of who she was pervades my spirit. Mom also had a kind of clothing fit for her Layton Road Walk, clothing for following after Jesus. Mom clothed herself in self-sacrifice for her family, in kindness to those who might have mistreated her, in gentle remembrance of everything that had to do with her children, in a driving motivation to please God through service to her family, her church, and her community, in unflagging love for her husband and daughters, no matter what ugly response she received. These were the clothes of my mother I longed to inherit. Mom clothed herself in good character. She clothed herself like Jesus.

I never wear the old gray beyond my back door, but I long to wear her legacy everywhere. And this is her legacy to me: the example of a godly and precious woman who stood faithfully beside me in her baggy t's, elasticized pants, and worn Sunday dresses and pointed me closer to the *haute couture* of heaven's wardrobe.

This is my inheritance, contained humbly in—one old gray sweater.

Encouragement for Your Walk

But is the "old gray" sufficient for the walk with Jesus? What should we wear when we walk with Him? *"Therefore, as God's chosen people, holy and dearly loved, clothe yourselves with compassion, kindness, humility, gentleness, and patience"* (Colossians 3:12). *"... clothe yourselves with the Lord Jesus Christ..."* (Romans 13:14). We should look like Jesus, not just talk like Jesus. Learning how to clothe ourselves in the character traits of Jesus involves prayer, Bible study, submitting to God's Spirit, and daily, consciously, "taking off" those things that do not please Him. Obedience to God figures large in divine wardrobe grooming. In fact, obedience should be the standard by which we pick every item we "wear." Do our actions (our clothes) shine a positive light on Him? Do they flavor the world both sweet and salty? But the only way to sort through the closet of our characters and choose what pleases Him is to read His manual for grooming our souls and our actions—His Word. Put on Jesus when you get dressed each morning.

Lord, open our eyes to the sins we have made a too frequent part of our lives, like a critical spirit, unkindness, selfishness, anger. Show us our sin in living color, so we can seek your forgiveness, take off the sin in confession to you, and walk in step with you in the full-dress uniform of a believer in love with you. Clothe us in your character. May the fruits of your Spirit be visibly worn and actively lived.

27. Friendly Faces

My mission in China began in June when I taught English in a summer camp and stayed through the summer to begin teaching in September at a public high school in Fuzhou city, Fujian province, for the year. It was 2001, and the school year began with horrendous terrorist attacks on America, causing significant apprehension. I wondered, *What will this mean for America, and will I ever be able to leave China?*

Seven months into my overseas stay, seven friends encircled a festive party table in a small town in Pennsylvania and sang "Happy Birthday" to me. Then each woman offered words of encouragement, "Hang in there! May your days be filled with joy. Be strong. Don't give up. If God is for you, who can be against you? Remember—we love you." Sitting slightly akimbo in the seat of honor with a cock-eyed hat, a pillow-stuffed body, pearls and feathers draped about a bedraggled house dress, I sat—in effigy. The guest of honor *in absentia* from the party was represented by a charming dummy.

I watched my birthday party from twelve thousand miles away.

Their video of the party arrived two weeks after the event. Sue, Donna, Lois, Sharon, Marilyn, Debbie, Elaine, and Eleanor sat around a table decorated with winter delights and finger sandwiches. Sue hosted the party. Her hospitality had become famous—beautifully set tables, charming décor, delightful games, creativity. I'd seen her do wonders with a lemon—make it a candle holder, a dip container, a frosted centerpiece. The camera zoomed in on favors, gifts, food ... and well-loved faces.

My son Trevor and his future wife Casie were invited to get in on the video, and they showed up with my cat Oreo, whose separation from his beloved owner for the year surely caused stress to his feline senses. Their presence in the video was a creative gift of love. Of course, I cried as everyone reminded me electronically of their love and God's faithfulness and care.

The video played on the television in my apartment at the school where I taught Spoken English to about one-hundred-seventy twelve to sixteen-year-olds.

By the time my January birthday rolled around, rapidly on the heels of Christmas and Thanksgiving, I had been in China for over half a year. The days began to feel like a fearful wilderness experience far from family and friends. Their birthday party-in-*absentia* with heavenly timing brought needed encouragement. The road felt lonely, but I knew "sweet friendship refreshes the soul."

In the Bible, David roamed through a wilderness called Horesh (1 Sauel 23:15-18). Perhaps the days in the wilderness became as dispiriting for him as my long months in China were becoming for me. God had called David to a special mission—to succeed Saul as king—but the journey had become a tight rope walk with death. Even with his six hundred fighting men, David felt alone and vulnerable as Saul combed every valley and cave to try to end his life. Enter Jonathon, Saul's son no less, soul-friend and encourager, who knew David needed his spiritual brotherhood.

What a sweet time Jonathon and David must have had in that fearsome place as they made a covenant of friendship before the Lord. David's heavy heart had to be lifted by Jonathon's presence and godly wisdom. "Don't be afraid," Jonathon reassured this mighty man of God. "You will be king over Israel, and I will then be second to you." Jonathon even forfeited his right to the throne of his father Saul to his friend David.

How blessed we are on our Walk when we have a Jonathon-friend who encourages us in our wilderness. How blessed we are if we can *be* a Jonathon-friend to someone. My friends back home in Pennsylvania soothed my heart with love in a birthday video. They gave me the courage to keep on going, to endure with gratitude and contentment and without complaint.

A covenant reunion in the hills of Horesh or an electronic birthday party in China are proof that we can get by in dark places with sweet encouragement from our friends and with heavenly reminders we do not walk alone in our wilderness.

Encouragement for Your Walk

"Therefore, encourage one another and build each other up, just as in fact you are doing" (1 Thessalonians 5:11). Find a Jonathon-kind of friend for your journey, one who walks in harmony with you and is headed in the same direction. Our Layton Walk must be characterized by encouraging friendships. Consciously plan each day to shower someone with encouragement. Be a Jonathon-friend.

Lord, please guide us to that heart friend with whom we can share the Walk's joys and sorrows. Help us to find friendships with others who love you, increasing the bond of godly relationships, advice, and wisdom. Give us the example and counsel of others who are walking with you faithfully. And guide us to those whom we can encourage and to whom we can be a Jonathon-kind of friend.

28. Letters Home

Dear Reader,

A brown cardboard storage box in my closet contains cards, letters, and notes I've received for the past sixty years.

I saved them because their messages were kind, or they came from special people. They struck a chord with me for a variety of reasons, and I've never had the heart to get rid of them through all these years. The box can no longer contain its bounty.

The recent influx of papers and letters from my Dad's life combined with mine to fill a good portion of the closet. Time to glean a few and toss the rest.

The result: I've spent hours reading and lost in memories. My grandmother's rounded, neat cursive, wishing me well. Dad's strong, bold handwriting with something humorous to share. Friends, some long gone, remembered by their handwriting even before I read the name. Cards from my boys when printing their names was a laudable feat. Every handful or so, there would be one from my mother, a prolific letter writer, even when she didn't have the time because she was a mother first, and we were at college or camp and needed to hear her encouragement. Her familiar severe right slant and unclear letters had me rereading and deciphering as her handwriting always did—letters to me at college, in China, from hers and Dad's new home in South Carolina.

I pictured those many hands I loved as they wrote with their arthritis or age spots or broken nails, and I heard their voices come to life on the page.

Finally, I landed on a thank you note from my mother in 1999. A thank you note from my mother. Whatever would the woman who gave me breath and met my needs for the first quarter of my life and beyond have to thank me for? But she did, and I've framed the card, her love, and her unforgettable handwriting.

Today, I answered some emails and sent a few texts, but there wasn't one memorable piece of handwriting among them. No cursive to reflect personhood, nothing worth framing, no picturesque reminders of a hand or a life. Just Times New Roman 12-Point type in featureless black and white.

Perhaps this implies enough about teaching our children cursive in elementary school. Like so many other things, memorable is being sacrificed on the altar of quick, fast, and modern.

For over thirty years my career involved teaching teens grammatical rules and proper writing style. Now, I am flabbergasted when I realize my texts are dashed off with incomplete sentences, without end marks, minus capitals and punctuation. Whatever happened to the Mrs. Walczak of eighth grade English class? Several generations of teenagers must be equally flummoxed about the years they spent learning English grammar that have been blown to the iCloud in social media.

Here's a challenge for those who dare to take it: let's return to the art of letter and note writing, even if only once a week—or month. How do we recover this lost art? Simply, do it. Pick a recipient who could use a bit of joy and scratch away. I realize it will cost a postage stamp, and the cost keeps rising, and it will take a bit of your time, but nothing speaks friendship and love more clearly. Consider it memory-making for someone, carving kind words into forever. A day is brightened, encouragement shared, when the mailbox produces an envelope with someone's handwriting, buried among the bills and advertisements. The message doesn't have to be so meaningful that it is saved for fifty years, but it can exude friendship and kindness, poignant enough to frame with your fingerprints and style embossed across its face.

Letter writing—a technologically simpler, less intimidating, more inspiring way to lift someone up.

The most life-changing letters I've ever read are compiled as epistles from the likes of the Apostles Paul, Peter, James, and John whose goal was to communicate the Word of God. Originally recorded on parchment or sheep skin, they stand witness for eternity to God's everlasting love, and each bears the very handprint of God.

That box of letters I've kept for sixty years? Most of them are still in the box and back in the closet. Who would have the heart to dispose of such memories and kindness? Not me. I will continue to pen in cursive, and I challenge you to enrich your connectedness with a handwritten letter.

Happy writing,
Your Friend on Layton

Encouragement for Your Walk

The easiest and simplest way to offer words of encouragement? A handwritten note. The four or five lines of kindness offered sincerely can transform a person's attitude and outlook. Your note may be the only word-hugs someone receives for a week. A noble purpose for life. A friend of my mother, Ruth Wills, wrote notes to her consistently from the time they graduated nursing school until my mom's death, and then Ruth wrote similar encouragements to my dad, my sisters, and me. She never missed a holiday or birthday. At Ruth's death, many people attested to her lifelong ministry of writing notes of encouragement—not only to the Joneses but to everyone in her sphere.

But the most powerful letter we will ever write to the world is the one "penned without ink." Paul wrote, *"You yourselves are our letter, written on our hearts, known and read by everyone. You show that you are a letter from Christ, the result of our ministry, written not with ink but with the spirit of the living God, not on tablets of stone but on tablets of human hearts"* (2 Corinthians 4:2-3). Living out Christ before the world, YOU are the most powerful letter anyone can receive. Live a life worthy of the high calling of being a child of God by walking like Jesus, following His way.

"Walking is not about what we are doing; It's about how we are living," wrote Lori Wilhite, founder of "Leading and Loving It," a ministry for Women in Leadership and pastors' wives.

Lord, keep us in your Word, learning of your character and actions. Help us to understand how to live like you. Help us to be a letter from you to the world—penned without ink.

Part 7
Around the World

I traveled the world last week.
Passports and visas were moot issues.
Flight delays and cancellations, non-existent.
Food, language, culture, and friendship,
abundant and rich,
during the week I traveled around the world
without leaving
Layton.

Jo Ann Walczak

29. Cultural Bridges

If you have ever watched the opening and closing ceremonies of the Olympics in China on television, you know the Chinese have a flair for spectacle, drama, and excess in productions that should make the producers of the Super Bowl half-time shows pale in comparison. And a show-biz extravaganza in China would highlight the 2001 school year at one Chinese high school.

December 31st and January 1st are holidays in America. Not so in China where it's business as usual. School is in session.

One year, on December 31st, 2001 at the Fuzhou Foreign Languages School in Fuzhou, China, students and faculty took a slightly different approach to the school day by celebrating not the New Year, but their "First Foreign Language Festival," which now continues to be an annual tradition.

Established by Irish missionaries at the turn of the 20th century, the Fuzhou Foreign Languages School lived through the end of the last Chinese empire, a civil war, the rule of Mao Tse Tung, a Communist takeover and the Cultural Revolution when teachers were often sent off for "re-education" in the countryside. In 2001-2002 their first native English-speaking American teacher, in the hundred years of their existence, took up residence at the school.

Her name was Miss Jones, an easy-to-pronounce English name compared to Mrs. Walczak as she was known in her high school back in Pennsylvania, where "Walczak" created pronunciation problems even for the best English speakers in a population of Polish surnames.

THE WALK ON LAYTON

The "First Foreign Language Festival" on December 31, 2001, was Miss Fang's brainchild. Miss Fang was the Dean of the English Department, my immediate supervisor, and a taskmaster in the best Chinese tradition. The festival's purpose was to cultivate the use of spoken English, encourage a spoken English milieu, and utilize its sole American teacher—me. English was one of only four required school subjects in China, primarily because speaking English provided an important way up the economic ladder.

Miss Fang oozed creativity. She planned the festival to be an all-day, all-school event for its two thousand students, a way to celebrate the "joys of speaking English," a concept that might warrant revival in America. She organized room decorating, games, and song competitions, but the highlight of the day was a two-and-a-half hour show for a packed house at a local cinema theater just a short walk up the Lu.

Miss Fang's show featured twenty student and teacher presentations: songs, poems, speeches, dances, and plays. From behind the stage curtain I watched, thoroughly impressed with the students' creativity and ingenuity. In fact, we weren't past the first number, and I knew I was out of my league. I could speak English, but I couldn't sing like Dolly or dance like Travolta. I started to fear I would be a woeful disappointment to Miss Fang, my mentor and friend.

Machines pumped fog across the stage for a troupe of students dressed as Japanese kimonoed dancers. Synchronized dance numbers featured fans and banners swinging in rhythm. Sixty ballroom dancers in gowns moved in perfect formation until I was ready to sashay out the back door of the theater and forget I had a part in the performance.

But the ever-present Miss Fang would not let her only native English speaker escape. She was at the door, in my face, and generally everywhere at once. Always smiling and bowing, this in-charge lady was a taskmaster, a workaholic, and a perfectionist, who had become one of my best friends in the four months I had been in her charge. Driven by love for the school and its students, she taught me much about the art of teaching and the joy of serving her school. Yet this diminutive pack of dynamite had nearly become my nemesis over the last few weeks.

Before Thanksgiving (a thoroughly American holiday not celebrated in China), I had a call from Miss Fang to report to her office, not an uncommon occurrence. "Jo Ann, we will be having a Foreign Language Festival at the end of December, and at the Festival I would like you to do two hours of English word games at English Corner in the courtyard, teach the teachers several songs in English to sing at the Festival, and perform a play with your spoken English class." She smiled ear-to-ear as she explained my task and then bowed the traditional three times as if to say, "Big job. Get to work. Make it great." Smiling, more bowing. My stomach churned for a month like the Chinese wringer washer on my apartment balcony.

Initially, the music seemed to be the biggest challenge. My only contribution to any choir had been volume, not melody. The teachers nixed several songs I chose as too difficult, including "Lean on Me" and "My Favorite Things." My knowledge of contemporary music came to an abrupt halt prior to my child-rearing years in the eighties, so current hits were not on my radar.

Fortunately, the Carpenters, Karen and Richard, although long past their prime in America, were making a big hit in China at the time,. Karen dominated every sound system in China's larger stores. So the teachers chose her hit "Sing a Song" as their first number. Both Chinese and Spanish language challenged, I was amazed by their choice of "Una Paloma Blanca" as their second number. My ability to provide either musical or language help immediately came into question. As with most of my other self-directives in life, my coaching amounted to this advice: "Sing loud. Smile big. They'll love you for your spirit." (A philosophy that has saved face for me on many occasions, and in China "saving face" is everything).

Those lovely, submissive Chinese teachers did whatever they were told, uncomplainingly. At the Festival they sang their hearts out, but most were too nervous to "smile big" because they concentrated intensely on remembering the words. Our performance did not take the show by storm, despite Miss Fang's efforts to add excitement by having glitter fall unexpectedly like a rainstorm from the rafters during our songs. A surprise to all of us, it served to break the focus of my Chinese colleagues who promptly forgot the words.

THE WALK ON LAYTON

But it was the play that dominated my attention in the month before the festival. Our American short story writer, O. Henry, appeals to the Chinese for his clever and ironic endings. I rewrote his story, "The Policeman and the Anthem" in seven short scenes of easy English. The story is about a homeless man in New York City who, faced with winter cold, tried his hand at a variety of crimes to get himself arrested and sent to a warm jail cell for the winter.

Our cast of twenty-five students practiced for an hour every day. Most students only had to learn three or four lines, except for "Soapy," the homeless man and the lead character in the show. I chose Allen for that part. His English wasn't the best, but he had mastered the art of class clown, almost unheard of in Chinese classrooms, and he was fearless about speaking up in class with his broken English, unlike most Chinese teens who cowed with embarrassment. But, best of all, he was loud, another uncharacteristic trait of Chinese students in the classroom.

Cherry, our narrator who spoke wonderful English, would become incensed with Allen's garbled English during rehearsals, and she would stop in her recitations to give him dirty looks and rail at him in Chinese. Who knows what she said, but her looks were venomous. Michael was a "reader," like a Greek chorus role. He turned out to be highly nervous and as the curtain on performance day was rising, he was yelling to me, "How do I say 'Enjoy, enjoy'?"

The play had five policemen. We were able to obtain authentic Chinese police uniforms from the husband of one of our school's teachers. Steven, Disney, Vince Carter, Jordan (Michael), and James were the biggest boys in the class. They received the coveted roles of policemen, and each brought his own brand of "police aura."

Vince Carter did a superlative job with his line, "Is there a problem here?" And Jordan's, "What are you doing here?" was convincing, though not entirely discernible. Steven had a wonderful swagger and gave a hearty laugh on cue, but his "Poor slob!" had too many p's and b's, and it ended up mostly spit. Disney couldn't get his lines out fast enough. He speaks English at record pace, and he managed to run on stage, spew out his lines and hustle off in a flash.

But our star, Allen, did a wonderful job. He managed to look perpetually cold on a snowy winter day, eat sloppily in a diner, and fall realistically when shoved around. If only he had remembered to turn on his lapel microphone.

The art teacher and the school carpenter had been dragged into the pre-show mix by Miss Fang, also. The carpenter made a sign for each store scene on our New York street, and the art teacher rigged up a window that dropped a giant crack when hit by Soapy's rock. Even the art department had challenges with my production. Barry, another of my students, worked with the art teacher on the staging, but he could not grasp the entire concept. Barry only knew "play" as something he did as a child.

These super Chinese teens put forth a great effort, despite the inabilities of the director. More than once I would forget myself and launch into a lengthy directive, only to discover my students were bleary-eyed and oblivious to my rambling English. They were patient with me and endlessly graceful.

But this marvelous New Year's Eve memory had a sequel almost two decades later.

In 2018 Allen, our Soapy, now in his early thirties and working for a Chinese corporation, came to Texas on business. He remembered his American "Spoken English" teacher at the Fuzhou Foreign Languages School who talked about Pennsylvania, her home. A few emails to old schoolmates, and Allen located me and made the trip up from Texas to visit in my home.

Nearly two decades and half a world later, Soapy showed up on Layton.

And he came to Layton with a message. He hadn't forgotten the "Soapy" of Fuzhou. Soapy, he said, had changed his life and given him the incentive he needed to develop courage, confidence, and personal strength to step out and speak up in his school and career. Allen knew if he could perform as the lead in a play, speaking a foreign language as a teen, he could do most anything with his life—and he has.

An unexpected event, a school play, brought success and hope to our main character. New years are like that. They can be the beginning of new grace and new hope. This was a satisfying resolution to a school play in China, worthy of O. Henry and characteristic of our Sovereign God who loves happy endings.

Encouragement for Your Walk

Take the challenges God offers along your path. Accepting an out-of-the-box opportunity sets us up for a more dependent relationship with God, a necessary pattern for life. He reminds us, *"... 'My grace is sufficient for you, for my power is made perfect in weakness.' Therefore I will boast all the more gladly about my weaknesses, so that Christ's power may rest on me"* (2 Corinthians 12:9). Stepping out for God in obedience is challenging and difficult. Plunged beyond our comfort zones, we falter, stumble, and, if our focus is clear, fall resolutely at the feet of Jesus where we utter the most essential prayer, "I will trust your sufficiency, Lord, for you are enough." He hears us, and He answers in ways we could never imagine.

Perhaps leaving your comfort zone on life's trek is helping in your local high school or traveling to the South to work with Habitat for Humanity or visiting new people in the neighborhood. Take courage. Step out of your world of comfort, and make "I trust your sufficiency, Lord" your cry of dependence and recognition of His sovereignty.

El Shaddai, obedience to you is our desire, but weakness and fear often control us. Grant us your strength to do difficult things and your courage to face scary obstacles.

30. A Trail of Breadcrumbs

Myth and folklore often have roots in truth.

The story of Hansel and Gretel reflects a truth I saw illustrated on one of our journeys across China. Germany, circa 1840. Famine grips the land, and Hansel and Gretel's stepmother determines to take the children deep into the woods and abandon them there so she and her husband will not starve to death. The brother and sister overhear the stepmother's plan. As the wicked stepmother leads the children through the woods, Hansel leaves a sprinkling of breadcrumbs to mark the trail and lead them home. When the wicked stepmother leaves the children deep in the forest, Hansel assures Gretel that God will not forsake them.

Eventually, they discover a cottage made of gingerbread, cakes, and candy, owned by a wicked and cannibalistic witch who uses the candy to lure children in and eat them. The witch tries to fatten up and cook Hansel and Gretel, but some quick thinking on Gretel's part lands the witch in the oven. The tables are turned. The wicked witch is dead. The children discover precious jewels in the house. They return safely home with the treasure for a happy reunion with their father and with the knowledge that their wicked stepmother is also dead.

A gruesome story with a victorious ending and a kernel of truth. China, circa 2015. Spiritual famine grips the land. Many people, lost in a dark forest of atheism and humanism, search for the way home to truth, love, a life of eternal purpose, a Father who loves them. But the evil one is prowling the forest, ready to devour them, luring them with sweet promises of power and glory. The forest looms, fearsome and foreboding. An oven awaits those who take shelter in the way of evil.

Home with their Heavenly Father means a rich inheritance of spiritual blessings and an ultimate victory over the wicked one. This is truth.

But how do today's generations find truth in this post-modern culture rampant with opinions, philosophies, dogma? How do they sort it out to find the truth? God's Word the Bible has stood the test of time, the test of credibility, the test of divinity, the test of human transformation. It contains truth.

Committed to its integrity and authority, we played Hansel and Gretel that summer, dropping bits and pieces of the "bread of life" or the Bible from east to west in China, leaving a trail to lead the wandering "home" to their loving Father. Far and wide, we scattered the "bread of life," in the form of mp3 audio devices called "Pathlighters" and "Wildlife Storytellers," from the East China Sea to the borders of Tibet.

Each mp3 contained God's words and powerful Bible stories. The children's audio was encased in a stuffed animal. The adult version was a hand-held, pocket size player. Neither were recognizable as banned materials. We spent three weeks, traveling east to west in China, distributing these valuable messages wherever and to whomever we could.

Like Hans' breadcrumbs, the Pathlighters and Wildlife Storytellers were collected by taxi, van, and bus drivers, fellow passengers, teachers, cooks, college students, twenty-something's, grandmas and grandpas, employees of large companies, street vendors, and children.

They found the "bread," sent to lead them home, kernels of truth about their heavenly Father's love for them and the sacrifice He made to save them from the wicked one. The Hansel and Gretel journey in China brought joy unparalleled to lost and seeking people.

Encouragement for Your Walk

Jesus declared, *"I am the bread of life. He who comes to me will never go hungry, and he who believes in me will never be thirsty ... whoever comes to me I will never drive away ... For my Father's will is that everyone who looks to the Son and believes in him shall have eternal life, and I will raise him up at the last day"* (John 6:35-

40). "Take my truth to the world," He asked us. Sprinkle your daily paths with "bread of life" truths from God for the people with whom you come in contact.

Father God, thank you for Jesus, the bread of life. May each bread of truth from your Word spread abroad and embed in the hearts and minds of others. Help us to share your Word through relationships, experiences, and conversations. Allow truths to blossom into faith as people begin to walk the road of life with You.

31. Surrounded

Every Walk sees its share of unforgettable milestone events and memories worth passing down through generations as legendary stories. Of course, Jesus had the attention of His disciples—and He gets ours because He loved to tell stories of the kingdom—through parables, metaphorical stories.

Have there been hair-raising moments on your Walk? Sounds in the darkness, footsteps nearby, specters reappearing around each bend of the road? Has life's road frightened you? Will your husband survive his cancer, and what would you do without him? Will your teenage son avoid the traps of alcohol and drugs, or will his life be squeezed into the cultural trends? Will you find another job and be able to pay the mortgage, taxes, and insurance without going into bankruptcy?

Traffic on our roads jams up with fear. How do we face those fears? Walking the roads in China sometimes fear ran rampant. On our tour bus near the farthest western border of China, Gao Yun coughed and sniffled her way to the front of the bus. From her vantage point beside the bus driver, she delivered a lengthy speech in Mandarin to the seated passengers. Her pronouncement complete, she left the bus and headed for her hotel room to sleep off the dregs of the flu.

After Gao Yun's departure, my friend Sharon's expression said, "Now what?" My other friend Marilyn's eyes grew as big as our morning noodle bowl. And I wondered what kind of a substitute leader I would be with a Mandarin vocabulary consisting primarily of hello, goodbye, where's the WC, and God bless you. Fear crept in.

A dear friend for many years, Gao Yun had asked us three visiting

Americans to join her on a trip to Dali, Lijiang, Chengdu, and the Tibetan foothills of western China where she intended to reconnect with former companions.

The only Americans on the bus tour, we had traveled hundreds of miles with this busload of vacationing Chinese. Together, we sailed scenic lakes on dragon boats that ferried passengers to botanical gardens while lute-playing musicians entertained below deck. We had hiked to butterfly gardens, through forests draped with Tibetan prayer flags, and over rocks that rose from the landscape like the teeth of behemoths. We'd visited the international panda bear breeding facility in Chengdu. We had eaten in Chinese noodle shops and in fast food restaurants where the usual seven courses were served in rapid succession—fast. Along with our tour companions we had elbowed our way, in typical Chinese tourist fashion, onto trains, planes, buses, and vans to get to this far-flung part of the world as far from home as we would ever be.

In awe and wonder about this country where God had brought us, I marveled again at the unexpected turns a Walk with the Savior might take.

Throughout our journey in China, Gao Yun was our only fluent English companion. The tour guides, who spoke only Mandarin, would perform wildly humorous presentations from the front of the bus about the history and geography of the region. I supposed the pantomimes involved history and geography. I supposed they were humorous, not because I understood what they were saying, but because these animated guides changed the tones and inflections of their voices, waved their arms dramatically, sometimes even donned a new hat or brandished an interesting prop, bringing the rest of the bus to laughter. But we had no idea what we were seeing in the vistas beyond the bus windows unless Gao Yun remembered to give us a play-by-play. Sadly, she had become progressively more tired and ill as the trip continued.

A standard rapport continued for days with our bus mates—smile often and nod wildly. Conversation, except with a few college students who wanted to practice their rudimentary English, was sparse and repetitive. Gao Yun, the touchstone with our bus companions and with the strange and unfamiliar world outside the bus windows, eventually left us to our own creative form of communication.

Holed up and ill for several days in the cocoon of her hotel bed, Gao Yun left us on our own to guess what we were seeing and doing. I supposed our best tack would be to follow the crowd closely and hope we didn't get lost or embarrass ourselves with cultural *faux pas* or make ourselves sick on oxtail, chicken feet, or snake.

One evening activity entailed a walk through Lijiang's old city—an ancient place of labyrinthine alleys, pagodas, cobbled roads, street vendors, and a plethora of souvenir shops where shopkeepers vied for our attention and money, sometimes refusing to let us pass by. The crowd pressed in on all sides. We held our bags close, wary of pickpockets. My phone had been "picked" previously out of my coat pocket, and I had no sensation of its being taken. Apprehension built as the three of us often held hands and became a bit too pushy in order to stay together on Lijiang's crowded streets. Getting lost here without directional knowledge or language was a tourist's nightmare.

At some point one of us noticed something interesting. About twenty feet behind, heads bobbing through the crowd, were a man and his wife from our bus. He had identified himself to Gao Yun as a politics teacher in a Chinese high school. As we made our way through ancient Lijiang, I would frequently glance behind, and the handsome couple hovered never too far behind us, though hidden by pedestrians. We couldn't lose them because they weren't losing us. Could they be following or watching us?

Then we recognized others from the bus—some to our left, some to the right, some even in front of us, all rather inconspicuous in the crowds but always trailing our circuitous route. For the remainder of the evening they seemed to continually have us in their line of vision, looking away when we looked at them, but following without any obvious revelation of their exact location.

I began to refer to them as our "border collies." Once on a visit to the highlands of Scotland, I watched the fast and powerful black and white border collies as they herded their flocks over the fells. If the sheep roamed too far right or left, the collies ran to that side to nip and bark them back to the group. The dogs could protect the clueless and stubborn sheep from harming themselves by stepping off a cliff or falling away from the safety of the flock. Our Chinese "border collies" often stood between us and a cliff, or worse.

A day or two later, when ailing Gao Yun recovered and joined us again on the bus, she explained the speech she had made to our bus companions on the day she retired to her hotel room for several days of recovery. "Please keep an eye on my American friends and help them," she'd said. "They may harm themselves or go somewhere they shouldn't. They don't speak Chinese. They will need your help." And our Chinese fellow passengers had complied. Never getting too close to cause us to wonder or question them but always remaining close enough to protect us, our friends had provided unseen protection and safety They would have stepped in to guide us like border collies if we had taken a questionable direction or entered the wrong kind of shop. We were secure in them, and we didn't even know it.

Secure and we didn't even know it—how often this describes a relationship with God. He is always present, always with His eye on us, never allowing us to wander beyond his sight and care. The prophet Isaiah reminds us, *"Whether you turn to the right or to the left, your ears will hear a voice behind you, saying, 'This is the way; walk in it'"* (Isaiah 30:21). And yet I often choose to go my own way, trusting my own instincts or wisdom, ready to step off a cliff rather than look to the One who knows the way, and failing to listen for His voice behind me.

Hearing God and knowing His presence takes time on the bus and on the road. We have to learn to communicate with Him because our native language tends heavily toward humanity rather than divinity. Time with God, our "tour guide" for the journey, and time spent getting to know the One who superintends this journey with us and loves us, will open our eyes to know His love and watchful care.

Whether in the ancient city of Lijiang, China, or in the fearful potholes of current relationships in American life, God promises to be near. He sends "border collies" of unknown identity to help. Behind us, before us, around us, God is there—in China, on Layton, or wherever you may be.

Encouragement for Your Walk

"You know when I sit and when I rise ... You discern my going out and my lying down. You are familiar with all my ways ... You hem me in behind and before and you lay your hand upon me. Such knowledge is too wonderful for me, too lofty for me to attain" (Psalm 139:1-6).

Recognize the hand of Your Creator and believe you are encompassed in His knowledge and care. Our relationship with the Father will bloom as we learn to walk with Him, *"whose glory ... is my rear guard"* (Isaiah 58:8). Our rear guard, a position He describes as glorious. The Bible, our guidebook for the journey, is clear: *"You will protect me from trouble and surround me with songs of deliverance ... the Lord's unfailing love surrounds the one who trusts in Him"* (Psalm 32:7,10). Walk strong and confident, for He is behind us, before us, with His right hand upon us

Father Protector, thank you for always watching us and providing defense and care. We are clueless often to the dangers of our paths and the temptations set by satan. Thank you for surrounding us with your love.

32. Orphanage Reunion

The metal entry door clangs shut. Children's artwork lines the walls of the entry hall. The ceilings vault over ten feet. Frequent mopping leaves water pooled on the concrete floors. The walls are two-toned, the bottom sporting an institutional green, topped with faded white. Void of furniture other than a long, low table and small chairs, the room echoes in the emptiness. Voices rise faintly from the television room and the upstairs bedrooms. Feet clatter, and, suddenly, twenty-four children appear, excited, laughing, gibbering away in Chinese with arms open to hug the arriving American grandmothers.

Once again the *ninis* (grandmas) arrive in Fuzhou, China, at the Living Hope Children's Home—a long way from Layton.

Beginning in 2004, the Living Hope children have drawn those grandmas across the world for seven annual visits. Bearing suitcases filled with English lessons, games, prizes, stickers, skit props, and craft projects, the grandmas settled down in China to do what grandmas do on every continent—talk, sing, laugh, tell stories, take walks, and hug. On our initial visit to Fuzhou in 2004 the children ranged in age from four to eleven.

In 2015 the grandmas returned again to Fuzhou, after a hiatus of several years, for a special reunion with the children who had run to meet them so often in the past when they had arrived from America, but the "little ones" weren't so little anymore. Teens and young adults greeted the ninis on this later visit, some with an outstretched hand, others with a hug.

Simon returned to the orphanage too. He was one of only two or three children adopted out from our original group of about twenty-two at the orphanage, due to unusual restrictions in Chinese law. Simon (Chinese name "Ming") had been adopted by an American family from the state of Washington when he was about seven-years-old. A pastor and his wife had three children of their own, but hearts big enough to include the adoption of two Chinese children, including Ming.

Eventually, Simon graduated from high school in America. His senior project, a ping pong tournament called "Ming Pong," raised over a thousand dollars to buy a ping pong table and other materials for his former orphanage home in Fuzhou. So the pastor from Washington brought Ming and the rest of their family back to Living Hope Children's Home in the summer of 2015, after Ming's senior year, to meet his "brothers and sisters" and "mommies and daddies" whom he had not seen since his adoption about eight years before. Simon's presentation of his "Ming Pong" gift to the orphanage would coincide with a reunion of his childhood "family."

Articulate, charismatic, and energetic, Ming is an adoption success story. After his high school graduation, he enrolled at Lancaster Bible College in Pennsylvania in September. It was an interesting twist to know that our Chinese grandson would eventually attend college in Pennsylvania. Ming's desire is to live a life of gratefulness, thanking and honoring God for His watchful care and love through his growing-up years at the children's home in Fuzhou.

Ben, another of our Chinese children, also came back for the reunion. Ben's crippled leg was just one of several obstacles he sought to overcome. He left the orphanage at eighteen and struck out on his own to experience the world and live the life he'd seen on television. Things did not go well, Ben said. At twenty-one years old, Ben admits he learned hard lessons about choices and the world's empty promises. He grew up fast.

Ben took a six-hour bus trip to spend a single afternoon with his "brother" Ming, his orphanage siblings, and the American ninis. And he wanted to tell those grandmas something special:

"You gave me some of the best memories of my childhood," Ben faltered. "As a child, I didn't understand the level of your commitment. I thought you came from nearby. I'm older now, and I know that you came a great distance. It cost you a lot of money and a lot of time and a lot of trouble."

Ben's hands and voice shook as he rose from his chair and invited the ninis into an adjoining, vacant room. Closing the door behind him, Ben lined the grandmas up, shifted his weight from his lame leg, and bowed deep and low to the older women. "I just want to say thank you. Thank you for your sacrifice for us. Thank you for the good memories." And he hugged each one of us, bringing all three ninis to tears.

Without a commitment to Jesus, we are all spiritual orphans, but Jesus promises, *"I will not leave you as orphans. I will come to you"* (John 14:18). When we commit our lives to Christ on our Emmaus Road, He gives us His Spirit, allowing us to become sons of God, orphans apart from God no longer. In Him, like the fatherless, we find compassion, comfort— Home.

Encouragement for Your Walk

When we meet Christ on an Emmaus Road and recognize and accept Him as our Savior and Redeemer from sin, we are adopted into the family of God. He gives us all the privileges of a family member: access to Him twenty-four hours a day, forgiveness of sins, unconditional acceptance, the presence of His Spirit in our lives to empower, strengthen and guide us, and an eternal home in heaven with Him. We have a new identity and a new relationship with Him who gives us the privilege of calling Him Abba, Father. We become a son or daughter of the Most High God.

"… he predestined us for adoption to sonship through Jesus Christ, in accordance with his pleasure and will—" (Ephesians 1:5). Be encouraged—you have been chosen by His pleasure and will.

Thank you, Abba, for adopting us into your family. Thank you for giving us a new name, child of God. Help us to live each day worthy of this high calling. Make us mindful of walking as you desire so your name is honored. We long to please you, Father.

"So in Christ Jesus you are all children of God in faith" (Galatians 3:26).

33. Potluck Hot Pot

The year of the monkey wiggled in on Monday, February 8th, 2002, signaling the first day of the Chinese lunar calendar and Chinese New Year. *Xiannian kuaile*! (Pronounced shin-nyen kwhy-ler). Happy New Year, Mandarin style.

Celebrating the new year in China is as easy as pulling your chair up to the table. It's all about eating with family and friends. "Hot pot" is the usual fare of the season. It reminds me of fondue, only trickier. The hot pot, or a boiling pot of water, sits on a portable burner and dominates the center of the table. The table must be circular as it's an equal opportunity conversation setting. Nothing goes better with hot pot than relationships.

The universal rule is, "Don't eat hot pot with people you don't like." That could have something to do with the double dipping and lavish exchange of saliva that takes place in the group pot. Everyone cooks and eats out of that one bubbling mix. Nothing spells unity like hot pot.

Bowls of just about anything surround the hot pot: mussels, greenery (of every shade and texture), chicken feet, rice noodles, oysters, squid, eel, fish balls, tofu, mushrooms, vegetables, and shrimp, all raw and fresh from the street market. Since my city in China was a coastal city, hot pot was always heavy in seafood. Shrimp are usually the most difficult to control on the table. Everything was "directly from the sea this afternoon" fresh, and the shrimp, alive and kicking, make a feisty delicacy.

During one new year's hot pot I attended, the shrimp took to jumping out of the boiling water on to the table whenever they were thrown in. Cooking them seemed almost barbaric, especially when they slapped you in the face in their attempts to escape. The chop sticks would start clicking and dunking around the table, and the shrimp never had a chance.

Once you throw your tofu into the pot, the next problem is finding it. Perhaps it sinks under a sea of bok choy and buries itself beneath the rice noodles. The natural impulse is to do a little "chopstick washing," swishing your chopsticks about in the broth to find your tofu. I tried that approach at first, but it appeared that rather than wash my chopsticks in the mutual eating pot, it was easier to just take whatever floated to the top and was handy. After all, you're among friends. Your fish ball is my fish ball.

Eastern culture values time around the table. Talking, eating, cooking, enjoying each other's company for several hours. These are the joys of the East. No rush. Another cup of tea. This is the essence of a Chinese New Year celebration.

The Eastern culture of Jesus' day was much the same. Although hot pot was probably not on the menu, there were mutual dipping dishes, and with all those fishermen friends, Jesus probably ate plenty of fish. He loved to share a meal with anyone—short tax collectors who sat in trees, good friends just off their boats, big crowds, wedding guests, families. Meal times were for relationship building. Dinners were a place to meet God.

How are meal times at your house? Hurried? Pressured? Eat and run? TV dinners or boxed mac and cheese? Mobile phones dominating the attention of everyone at the table?

Maybe a hot pot is in order.

Cook together around a gurgling pot. Laugh about missing mushrooms and feisty shrimp. Engage in a chop stick battle over the last noodle. Get to know each other a little better.

A hot pot dinner reminds me of one of those times God talked about teaching our children to love Him with all their hearts, souls, and strength. He said to impress this command on the children when we sit at home, when we walk along the road, when we lie down or get up, or—when we have family hot pot night.

Encouragement for Your Walk

"Love the Lord your God with all your heart, with all your soul, and with all your strength. These commandments that I give you today are to be on your hearts. Impress them on your children. Talk about them when you sit at home and when you walk along the road, when you lie down and when you get up" (Deuteronomy 6:5-7). God speaks clearly in His Word about family time and teaching time with the children. Our Layton Walk needs to allow plenty of interaction with children, especially, concerning God's love and watchcare over them and His desire to forgive their sins. They are the next generation. The gospel and God's values must be a part of their upbringing. Consequently, be sure your journey is filled with children and grandchildren, nieces, nephews, neighbors. Their company provides valuable teaching moments, times to share our love for Jesus, our faith in His promises, and His life-giving words, opportunities to encourage and uplift. Shower these precious ones with kindness and reminders of our love and God's love.

Abba Father, thank you for the multitude of children we encounter on the Walk. Let our love for them be obvious in the things we say and do. Empower us to share your Word with them and love them well. Let kindness be our action word.

34. Celebrations

Christmas punctuates the roads of our lives every year. For some, the holiday may be challenging. For others the holiday becomes the centerpiece of our year's events.

Cutting a fresh pine tree for the living room, caroling at the neighbors' or at a nursing home, visiting Nana and Grandpa Jones near Justus Corners, eating Aunt Betty's annual spritz cookie favorites, watching for reindeer to fly overhead and humoring Dad that we could see them, listening for Santa's bells, joining our Justus friends at the Mt. Bethel Church Christmas program, sitting on Santa's lap at church and trying to guess if it was really Jim Carpenter or Albert Morcom, entertaining Mama, Pa, Aunt Sally and Aunt Nancy every year on Christmas Day with dinner and games, and rereading the old story of a child named Jesus born as a gift of love from God—these have been among my favorite Christmas memories for over sixty years on Layton Road in Justus.

The memories are simple and true, and only some of the characters have changed as time marches relentlessly from Christmas to Christmas. The sameness and constancy of these Rockwell holidays comfort and encourage because it is what I expect and desire. God willing, I look forward to many more of these old-fashioned country Christmases that herald the birth of a Savior with accompanying joy.

Ironically, the Christmas that made me most appreciative of this holiday on Layton did not happen there. Oddly, although seventy-four of my seventy-five Christmases had been spent on Layton, it was that one Christmas *off* Layton that increased my thankfulness for Christ, home, family, Pennsylvania, America, and this special holiday.

It was 2001, and I was teaching spoken English in a public high school in southeast China for a year.

The school year had a traumatic beginning as I watched the destruction of the World Trade Center from twelve thousand miles away. I wondered if world war would ensue, and I would have to spend the rest of my days in China. The day after 9/11, a delegation of men from the PSB (Public Security Bureau, the CIA equivalent) came to my school apartment to investigate the premises. Was the apartment safe? Would I be sufficiently protected? As the only American in their section of the city, they were determined to see that I was free from any attacks on Americans. They shook the barred windows, checked the locks, surveyed the balcony, and pronounced me secure. Of course, one of them was assigned to keep "tabs" on my whereabouts. As an American, I was not used to such attention from the government. What would life be like for me in a Communist country and in a Communist school? "You're not on Layton anymore!" I reminded myself daily.

As the days grew into months, my apprehensions waned, and I fell in love with my Chinese students and my peers on the Chinese faculty. We studied and worked together, and our mutual interest in each other's lives and countries provided the fodder for growing friendships. By the time December rolled around, I was hopeful that these new relationships would provide the "family" atmosphere we American Christians so crave during our most precious holiday, Christmas. I was not disappointed.

I felt sure that the way to approach Christmas in this Communist country was in the American way—with a party. In fact, three parties were planned. Over sixty people attended my parties, and, unbelievably, not one of them had ever celebrated Christmas. What a privilege for me to be the bearer of great good news.

The first celebration with my students was to be a tree-decorating event, but like everything else in China for me, preparing for it became problematic. A live Christmas tree was nowhere to be found in this city of five million people. In fact, live trees of any type were few and far between in this concrete metropolis. Eventually, I located some artificial trees that would more correctly pass as large branches. Grudgingly, I settled for the artificial variety, quite a compromise from someone whose son is a forester and who has always had free access to a Christmas tree farm.

On party night about twenty of my sixteen to seventeen-year-old students came to set up the tree. I gave them the boxed tree and trimmings, and they went at it. A friend on Layton had sent along some Christmas cut-outs which bedecked the tree. The lights ended up primarily around the top, some branches had three ornaments, and the tree leaned treacherously to one side, eventually collapsing entirely. It only took a few slabs of that marvelous travelers' aid, silver duct tape, to secure it to the floor. The tree stood magnificently in its lop-sided, glittering glory. The students' oohs and aahs were heartening. We sang Christmas carols, and I served chicken noodle soup; you can never make a culinary mistake when you serve noodles at a Chinese party. Then the teens just sat and stared moon-eyed at the tree. Imagine giving young people their first opportunity to experience Christmas.

The second celebration was a "Neighbors' Night," to which I invited friends in the school apartment building where I lived. They had helped me to find the street vegetable markets, to operate the manual washing machine on my balcony, to locate the only English-speaking television channel (available only between the hours of 5-7 p.m.), and to instruct me in proper garbage disposal (toss it all in a heap behind the building where a little old lady with a pull cart will pick it up each day).

With the few improvised decorations available, I set the table in my tiny dining area. Christmas napkins and candy canes (neither of which could be found in Chinese stores) had been sent to me by friends in Clarks Summit. I lit a plethora of candles to create an atmosphere; the local Buddhist temple shop on my street was always well-supplied with an abundance of red candles. When my neighbors entered the apartment, they literally stopped in their tracks and audibly gasped as their eyes roamed from the Christmas tree to the table with all the wonder of our children on Christmas Eve.

Alarmingly, one of the men began to jabber away in Chinese and raced at breakneck speed out of the apartment and back down the steps. "What cultural *faux-pas* had I committed now?" I wondered. Within minutes he was back with his camera. What followed would have made Hollywood's paparazzi proud: photos of each individual in front of the tree, of each neighbor with the *mei gua ren* (American), and eventually of family groups.

By the time we sat down to Christmas dinner, it was a bit congealed. Beef stew (who knows why I chose stew as the entrée because it contained neither rice or noodles) was less than their favorite. I could tell because the women launched into a vigorous conversation (remember none of them spoke English) in very loud tones while picking through the stew, gesticulating, and leaving a good portion of it on their plates. Turkey (unheard of in China) and ham (only available in small chunks) were out of the question because locating an oven was problematic. No one had an oven. The wok ruled as the most important kitchen appliance. My dinner's salvation was the deviled eggs and Jello, another import from Clarks Summit friends. These were real crowd pleasers.

The "feast" was followed by table talk, such as it was, through my Chinese English teacher friend who had volunteered to translate. Hai Rong could barely get a morsel in her mouth through the course of the evening as everyone demanded her services. I asked a question to spur table conversation, "What was the best gift you have ever received?" After they shared, I told them of my "best gift" made possible by the very first Christmas.

The American party atmosphere persisted as I plunged into my third celebration for the Chinese English teachers on the faculty. Thirty-five Chinese were responsible to teach English in this high school of three thousand students where English is one of the four required subjects. I was the school's lone native English speaker so I was an in-demand novelty, bombarded daily with "How do you say this?" "What is the correct grammar construction?" "What does this mean?" They had a bottomless thirst for knowledge of all things English and American.

Nevertheless, my culinary skills and the Chinese markets prevented me from attempting another American Christmas dinner experience in my tiny apartment. I enlisted the *lo ban* (boss) of the school cafeteria to help. He cooked a Chinese luncheon that the faculty would relish, and I would make dessert, which was usually watermelon in their culture. Apple pie, cheesecake (the challenge was finding cream cheese and an oven), Jell-O, and cookies were cranked out of my tiny kitchen for the event, and, evidently, they were a hit as the Chinese took to American desserts like chopsticks to noodles.

Christmas is not a holiday in China, school is not cancelled, and I was still scheduled to teach two classes on Christmas morning. Thoughts of Christmas morning away from the family left me sad, but in the flux and turmoil of the post-9/11 world and in this Communist country on that Christmas, 2001, it was a security and hope to know that the message of Christmas will never change, no matter what happens, no matter where we are.

A name for Jesus is "Emmanuel, God With us." Emmanuel—with us wherever we are, even if the place we are does not acknowledge or recognize the reason and meaning of the season.

Back on Layton, I am preparing for another traditional Christmas this year made even sweeter by students and friends on the opposite side of the globe. Blessed Christmas, wherever you are.

Encouragement for Your Walk

In what lonely place are you? Is the lunchroom at work a difficult atmosphere? Do the ugly gossip and backbiting at school cause you to retreat from others? Is even your home sometimes a solitary place? You may not be in China, but fear and apprehension isolate. In those lonely, desolate places, even there, God is present. Dark shadows, created by isolation, cause the road we walk to encroach and smother. We feel alone. Stop and remember God's promise, "I will never leave or forsake you." We are never alone. Emmanuel, God with us, walks every step by our side. Remember and give thanks for His presence with you in that lonesome place.

Emmanuel, the forests sometimes darken our vision on the road. Frightening specters steal among the trees, and we are afraid. Help us to remember your promise of presence and live to that reality. Strengthen and embolden us to stand strong under your watchful care.

35. So Far Away

Christmas 2001. I awoke alone in a foreign country to a gray morning and a cold apartment, devoid of gifts, festivities, and companions. Loneliness and isolation reigned.

I pictured my family celebrating Christmas on the opposite side of the globe: the breakfast buffet, coffee flowing freely, gifts stacked high in piles around a well-decorated pine, carols on the stereo, scattered gift wrap, pajama-clad relatives, laughter. I tried to shake thoughts of family and prepared for my 8 a.m. class.

Teaching English in China had required a riveted focus on the One who called me to serve there. Challenges with language, food, and culture, although often frustrating, nevertheless, became exciting because God revealed Himself through His work and His presence. As I taught my classes and lived among the Chinese as the only American in my corner of a city of five million people, I relished the comfort and joy of Jesus' sweet whisper to me daily, *"The Lord himself goes before you and will be with you; he will never leave you nor forsake you. Do not be afraid; do not be discouraged"* (Deuteronomy 31:8).

God's desire for us to know His presence is evidenced everywhere in Scripture. On the first page of the New Testament His desire became flesh. The baby Jesus, Emmanuel, is born. His life from the manger to adulthood emphasized His driving passion: to be in relationship with people, to be with us.

But this Christmas morning as I walked to my classes in China, my focus slipped from Jesus and His presence. I wallowed in self-pity, and I prayed, "Lord, help me to know you are with me today. I miss my family. I feel alone. I am so far away from them." Christmas is not a national holiday in China. Life goes on as usual.

Even in mid-winter, the windows and doors of the classroom are open—something about good health and fresh air. Winter teaching garb included a coat and gloves. Feeling very alone and isolated from my family and the life I knew and loved on Layton, I hiked rather morosely to my 8 a.m. class. As I approached the classroom door, it was closed. *Now, what could this mean*, I wondered. Not only that, silence reigned—an almost impossible atmosphere when all of my classes had at least 60 students. Did I miss some directive from the headmaster? Possible. He only spoke Chinese so I missed quite a bit.

I pushed the classroom door open. It looked like all sixty were present, but the usual friendly chitter chatter was absent, and all eyes looked in my direction. Oh-oh! Had someone broken a desk or torn down a sign? Their smiles broke into laughter, and they pointed to the corner of the classroom.

And then I saw it. In the front corner of the classroom was a Christmas tree, a live one (wherever did they find it?) of at least ten feet in height, and it was covered with lights and decorations. I gasped, and the pent-up emotion of the day was unleashed. A typical Chinese person would find such a display of emotion a "loss of face," but being American, I blubbered away in the beauty and love of the moment. The children had secretly handmade every ornament on the tree in preparation for Christmas, a holiday they did not understand and had never celebrated. Again, in that Chinese classroom I heard His sweet whisper, "Dear child, I am Emmanuel. I am with you."

I don't know that any English language was taught that day, but I know that I received an incredible gift of love from these dear people as far from my home on Layton as I could possibly be.

Are you lonely?

Listen. Emmanuel is whispering, "You are not alone. I am with you wherever you go."

Encouragement for Your Walk

"The virgin will conceive and give birth to a son, and they will call him Emmanuel (which means 'God with us')" (Matthew 1:23).

Assigned to lead God's people into the Promised Land after Moses' death, Joshua was afraid. He had led battles, journeyed through the wilderness, seen God's miracles, but entering this foreign land, peopled by a strange, new nation, set his heart to fear. But God infused Joshua's heart with confidence when He promised, *"I will be with you. I will never leave you nor forsake you … Be strong and courageous … Do not be afraid, do not be discouraged for the Lord your God will be with you wherever you go"* (Joshua 1:5, 9b). God's promise is reiterated in many places throughout Scripture. It is a truth to be engraved in our hearts, a truth He wants us to remember.

On Christmas morning in China God proved, yet again, His faithfulness by His presence. These children did not understand Christmas, its meaning or significance, but God had prompted their hearts to live love to a foreigner. God acts and works even in the walls of a Communist public high school.

Lord, remind us daily that you tabernacle with us. When I gather my tent and move from comfort to fear, when I pull up stakes and travel from security to risk, you are still with me. Prompt us to remember that you walk every step of the way with us … wherever we may go.

36. Great Adventures

My "Great Adventure" in China ended when I pulled into my driveway on Layton at two in the morning one summer day after a door-to-door journey of about twenty-four hours. It's a long way, geographically and ideologically, from Yunnan and Tibet to Layton Road. Our adventure included scaling a precipitous mountain to a Tibetan village of eighteen families, bouncing along on a rock-strewn dirt road between Sichuan and Yunnan, minus guard rails and mindful of a thousand-foot drop into a river, bobbing about in a seafood shack in a bay of the East China Sea, walking through the street fires of a folk celebration at the Lijiang Fire Festival. Truly, adventure.

Sleeping away the twenty-plus hours of flying time during the long return from the other side of the world helped in re-acclimation, but nothing reorients a mind to the realities of Western culture better than Hollywood.

So, I attempted to regain my cultural "legs" by selecting an in-flight animated movie called UP! Inadvertently, UP! had me contemplating the nature of "adventure" rather than laughing at an old man's bumbling efforts to get to South America.

Carl Fredrickson, the movie's main character, married his childhood sweetheart, Ellie. They shared the mutual desire to follow in the steps of the great explorer Charles Muntz. In his dirigible, the *Spirit of Adventure*, Muntz had discovered Paradise Falls and a variety of exotic creatures in South America. Ellie and Carl made it their life-long dream to eventually visit Paradise Falls. In fact, Carl promised Ellie they would do it.

But life happened. The Fredricksons had to borrow from their trip savings account to pay for tires, house problems, and health issues, and in less than five minutes movie time the couple aged, Ellie died, and the dream adventure was lost. Carl sat glumly on his front porch, a bitter old man wondering where time had gone and regretting the adventure had never taken place. And then, in a surprising turn of events, he managed to get to Paradise Falls after all.

The crux of the movie comes when Carl discovers Ellie's scrapbook *The Spirit of Adventure*, and he sees the photos she pasted in the "Stuff I'm Going to Do" section. The photos chronicled their daily life together: marrying, setting up house, picnicking, sitting together in their easy chairs. Carl realized they *had* lived the adventure—every day, the adventure of a satisfying marriage and life together.

This past month in China had all the elements of Great Adventure: foreign places, strange food, intriguing people, exotic cultures, but it was the adventure of a lifetime, not because of those things, but because it was an adventure planned and orchestrated by God for His purposes and His glory. Sightseeing and exploring were secondary. An adventure with God is not limited to these special foreign "mission" trips. Watching God do a work in people's hearts—this is life's Great Adventure.

Like the Fredricksons, we can live the adventure every day. A prayer for God to use us doesn't have to happen on a mission field or in a land faraway. Great Adventures don't have to wait for Paradise Falls, South America, or Yunnan, China. Great Adventures for God can happen right here, right now, even on a road called Layton.

Reflecting on this, I realized the greatest adventure of life is the decision to follow Jesus Christ. The adventure begins on that Emmaus Road when Jesus is recognized as your Savior Redeemer … and then the climb toward our true home begins.

Encouragement for Your Walk

God's people had to learn how to live a Great Adventure with God on the road, again and again. They failed frequently. As a new nation, redeemed out of Egypt, Israel roamed for forty years through deserts and wilderness, experiencing a freedom designed to groom them into people who honored God and reflected His character to the nations they encountered. But this was no easy road. They failed frequently. Wars and rumors of wars encompassed their trek.

God schooled the Israelites to understand how to walk with Him, how to face daily difficulties, how to live victoriously when the scales seemed to tip against them, how to come into a relationship with Him. These were adventures of a divine nature. But the Israelites failed to obey God countless times; they failed to do what He asked them to do. They worshipped a golden calf statue they had made rather than the one true and living God. They complained about the food and rebelled against their leaders. Their great adventure on the dusty wilderness roads with God was unfaithful, idolatrous, and disobedient. They were left behind, never able to enter the Promised Land.

On this wilderness walk over dusty, pot-holed roads, how is the Great Adventure with God going for you? Are you trusting Him in every situation? Are you following God's commands for right living? Are you pursuing Him even when you see roadblocks up ahead? *"Submit yourselves then to God. Resist the devil, and he will flee from you"* (James 4:7). Don't play into the world's and the devil's ball park by sinning. A Great Adventure requires unflagging obedience to God's desires and a heart and soul love for the One who has prepared the way.

Father, help us to be obedient to your directions and calls. We are weak, and we fail frequently. Give us wisdom and understanding to see how the devil may be tempting us from your way. Grant us courage to do what you want us to do, to go where you want us to go, to walk away from sin.

Part 8
Shiny Days

LORD OF THE HIGHWAY

"A Christian may have entered the Valley of Humiliation overconfident and puffed up with false pride, but he departs with humble reliance on the Word of God and prayerful gratitude to the Lord of the Highway who has come to his aid and saved him from the Destroyer. He goes forward with his sword drawn. He has learned his lesson and now relies consciously on God's Word for protection."

John Bunyan
Author of The Pilgrim's Progress

37. Dance Along the Way

Sometimes on your Walk with God, I hope you dance.

Dance is an outward expression of the wonder, joy, and thankfulness we experience on life's journey, no matter what path life may take, no matter the ecstasy or sorrow. It is unified motion, flowing across time and space. Dance streams smoothly to the beat of the music and the thudding of hearts. It moves in rhythm and harmony with someone else. Dancing. I love it.

My dancing days date back to the early 1960s when we spent every lunch hour of our high school years spinning records in the school gym, jitter bugging with Elvis and the Beach Boys and twisting with Chubby Checker. Dancing provided a release from schoolwork and the limited scope of life in a country village. When we danced to the Beatles, Bobby Vinton, or the Four Aces, we weren't in rural Pennsylvania. We were in New York, London, or on the beach in California, and we were free, dancing to the beat of a different drummer.

My dance partner was Linda. She knew exactly how to lead, and I could easily sense and follow the nudges, pushes, spins and push-offs that she intended. We moved together flawlessly, almost floating in sync across the gymnasium floor.

Since high school, I haven't danced much, other than the occasional wedding. I did take a few turns with a professional ballroom dancer on a cruise once, but he seemed to demand more in movement and synchronization than I could muster. I tripped over his feet and my own with no inkling or sensation about which way I should step. The end of the song didn't come soon enough. Frustrated with my uncoordinated moves, I gladly exited the dance floor and headed for my seat, which I kept for the remainder of the evening.

But even that unsuccessful experience hasn't quenched my desire to dance. When I watch the show "Dancing with the Stars," the old desires rush to the fore, and I fantasize, envisioning a slim and youthful me dancing with Max Chmerkovskiy, a former star of the show, following his every guided movement, twirling across the stage, leaping, bending, spinning—a light and ethereal me, never stepping on his feet or mine, snapping my legs and arms to each orchestrated crescendo of the fox trot, rumba, tango, waltz, or *passe double*, gasping as Max flips me air born.

Alas, my imagination runs amok. My over-sixty, overweight body will surely never see this fantasy materialize unless I make it my goal to learn and practice diligently the skills of dancing. That probably won't happen. These days, my dancing is confined to my kitchen with Alexa's golden oldies, a dust cloth, and my vacuum, not with Max. It would appear to be the demise of dance for me.

Fortunately, I am learning to dance a different type of step.

In Galatians 5:25, God reminds us, *"Since we live by the Spirit, let us keep in step with the Spirit."* To keep in step with the Spirit, to sense His tender touch and to walk, move, speak and act in tandem with His Spirit—not to flail and stumble without grace through life, but to know the touch of the Master's hand gently nudging me in the right direction, to sense His leading and to stride in synchronization to His will, to rest in His encircling arms, and to step resolutely across the floor until the music ends. This is the dance I am learning. This is the dance I've come to love.

When I invited Jesus into my heart, He gifted me with His Spirit (Acts 2:38). My body became His temple. Now, God desires I walk and live with and through His Spirit. Sometimes a bump, shove, or a push, like Linda would have given me back in the sixties, is needed to point me His way. But always the loving gentleman, He is teaching me the art of listening and moving in harmony with Him.

How do we dance in sync with God's Spirit? By asking for daily cleansing from sin, by continually surrendering to His authority and leading, by listening for His still, small voice and nudge. My skills improve with consistency and faithfulness. I find myself longing to hear the sound of His movement because that will mean the Lord has gone out in front of me, and I need only follow His lead.

King David knew how to dance. In Psalm 149:3 God reminds us to *"praise his name with dancing,"* and David took every opportunity to do just that. When the Israelites brought the Ark back to the city of David, he *"danced before the Lord with all his might"* (2 Samuel 6:14). He danced with enough gusto to set the teeth of his wife Michal on edge. She despised his joy, jealous of the relationship he had found with God.

This is the dance I want to accomplish—listening for His Spirit in the tops of the poplars as He marches with me along the road, moving in tandem with His desire and will, and stepping to the sound of His music. Who knows? Perhaps I, too, can follow God's lead triumphantly for the entire dance, from Gibeon to Gezer.

And I pray this for you also—I hope on your road you dance.

Encouragement for Your Walk

"Since we live by the Spirit, let us keep in step with the Spirit" (Galatians 5:25). "Keeping in step" involves moving in rhythm and harmony with someone else. We must pursue a relationship with God through prayer and His Word to know how to move in harmony with Him on our Walk. And we will have those days, with our eyes Godward and our minds focused on Him, when we can skip and dance down our roads with joy and the assurance of His love.

Lord, help us to learn the dance of the redeemed by keeping in step with your Spirit. Teach us to acknowledge and respond to the joy of walking life with you. Help us to be faithful about talking with you and learning about you, so that kicking up our heels will be the most praiseworthy thing we can do.

38. Simple Joys

Some days of my Layton Walk overflow with simple joys.

But not usually on mornings. Mornings can be a slow slog. The usual routine—pajamas askew, hair disheveled, slippers shuffling, I maneuver down the steps from the upstairs bedroom and head directly to the front window in the living room. The point is to open the curtains and get the big picture window view of what the world looks like on Layton today. Is the sun beaming? Is there fog on the mountain or rain in the valley? Will the state of the weather predict the course of the day?

Unfailingly, this is the routine. Throw open the curtains on the world's stage, breathe deeply, scope out the day's prospects, and pray for the courage and strength to see it through.

One day, my usual routine took a lovely turn. Pulling back the curtains did not present me only with a view of Frankie's garage across the street and the mountain behind. The day's opening curtain call proved as exciting as a Broadway musical in its first thrilling notes. On the stage of my front lawn stood a buck, antlers held high, majestic and peaceful. Sensing my presence and staring back at me, he froze, and so did I. Our eyes met, but he remained motionless. I searched the area for the rest of his family. There were no other deer in sight, only this magnificent creature. Shortly, he grew bored with me, but he never ran. He stuck his head deeper into the nearby vegetation for another bite of his morning meal, and then he strolled calmly away into the woods, leaving me breathless at the window.

How can a day not begin with gratefulness when it starts with such beauty?

Some days, God just keeps those simple joys flowing.

With the spectacle of a front yard buck on my mind, I went about my morning activity: put coffee on, feed the cat, dress. But a steady buzzing drew my attention. Was one of the neighbors mowing already? Or was someone using their electric clippers to trim bushes? Was there something wrong in the basement? My directional hearing is not accurate. The buzz seemed to encompass the house like a giant mosquito, and it was incessant. The sound drew me to the back porch where it became obvious the noise originated overhead.

Incredibly, an aerial circus claimed the skies. A small plane dove, twisted, and spun high above my house. I pulled up a yard chair in the driveway, and, head back, I enjoyed the show. The pilot was wild with enthusiasm. He'd climb straight up, turn with his nose to the earth, and spin down until I thought he would join me for morning coffee. Back up he rose to a horizontal flight pattern, and he spun like the Salt and Pepper ride my grandchildren love at Knoebel's. What an acrobatic show, right here in my backyard on Layton. Later that day, I learned that my acrobatic pilot was practicing for an air show at our local airport.

God fills our lives daily with simple joys. Our heads may be full of worries and busyness that block our sight, but God asks us to change focus and "Give thanks in everything." He reminds us to live eyes and ears wide to the blessings around us and to give thanks for each one. No matter what difficulties and hardships we face, there are always things for which we can be thankful. Our lives abound with blessings, awaiting our recognition and appreciation.

The marvelous thing about thankfulness is that it opens the door to joy. Joy rushes in naturally right behind thanksgiving, and then contentment with life has its foot in the door.

Eyes and ears wide. Can you see many things for which you can thank the Creator on your Walk? I'm working on making it a habit here on Layton. Want to join me?

Encouragement for Your Walk

A key to the Walk is training ourselves to find joy each day and lavishing those joyful moments with thankfulness. In fact, in everything give thanks, for thanksgiving is the harbinger of contentment. We live in a discontented culture where almost anything is reason for complaint. "Nothing is as I'd like it," many bemoan. Is it difficult to see any joy in some days? Develop this valuable discipline to honor God on your Walk—give thanks in everything (there must be something!) and watch your joy and contentment grow.

I used to play "I Spy" with the children. Walk through your day with this refrain: "I Spy something I want to thank you for, Lord. It is …"

Father, thank you for the big and small blessings of each day: a hot cup of coffee in my warm living room, a job and purpose to fulfill, a refrigerator with food, a text from my son, an aerial show in the backyard, and a buck on my lawn. Help me to walk with the intent of spying your goodness. You are a gracious and kind God. Thank you for drawing me into Your family.

39. Everyday Miracles

Miraculous moments can happen every day if we are open to seeing them.

Today was one of those days.

The magic surprised us in the Wilmington, North Carolina, airport. Any random place can spawn miracles.

Dad drove me to the airport to get a flight back to Pennsylvania after a week with him in Little River, but the plane, long delayed, left us with several hours of waiting time. I took to people-watching in the airport lounge while Dad settled onto his phone and a few of his favorite games.

A young soldier in dress uniform caught my eye. Seated on the sofa across from us, he was hard to miss. Over six feet tall and handsome, his demeanor belied his appearance. His fingers tapped endlessly on his knee, on his chin. He wiped his brow. His leg vibrated up and down. I thought perhaps he had just returned from the war; perhaps this was Post-Traumatic Stress Syndrome. His nervousness continued for about an hour, and then a flight arrival announcement bolted him from his seat. Obviously, it was the flight number he was awaiting. He ran over to the door of the exit hall, a bouquet of flowers in hand, and he continued wiggling his hands and swaying from leg to leg like my six-year-old grandson.

As he stood by the gate and watched the disembarking passengers, his tension grew. He would look down the exit ramp and pace a short distance. Finally, he spotted someone, and he became quite still. I was eager to see the person he expected. What could possibly have made him so nervous?

A perky, petite cutie with a crop of curly blond hair came through the gate. She was a vogue picture in her pink and white sundress with a matching bag and sandals. Our soldier grabbed her and quickly wrapped his arms around her. A momentary kiss and a few quiet words ensued. Then, he dropped to his knee, all six feet of him, and he took her little hand in his. All of this in about three minutes.

"Look, Dad!" I elbowed my father wildly, but Dad was lost in a chess game on his phone. "Look!" By this time the entire lounge had zeroed in on the life-moment unfolding before us.

The poor guy probably couldn't wait until they got to the car. The entire lounge heard our soldier say, "Will you marry me?" His nerves had strengthened his voice. A small box came out of his pocket. Our heroine yelled, "Yes!" and a ring was immediately placed on her finger. Our soldier stood, lifted both arms to heaven (and the arrivals lounge clientele) and boomed, "She said, 'Yes!'"

Of course, we spectators couldn't get enough of this real-life movie scene. The delayed and frustrated lounge entourage forgot their annoyance with airlines, and we all burst into wild applause and whistles. Everyone in the lounge smiled, and the clapping continued.

The bride-to-be jumped into his arms, and there was a twirling and hugging in the middle of the lounge worthy of a Fred Astaire and Ginger Rogers movie. More applause. Some hoots and "atta boy's." Joy all around.

Quickly, the couple moved off toward the exit. The moment had united the rest of us. No doubt, everyone's memories traveled to the days of their own marriage proposals, weddings, or long married life journeys since then.

And everyone smiled—for the hope of newness and fresh starts and young love.

"She did everything right, " Dad remarked finally surfacing from his game in time to see the action. "She even lifted her leg when he picked her up." Who would have thought Dad was an expert in romantic protocol? A coquette indeed. A magical life moment shared by a room full of strangers.

The "magic" continued. With a farewell to Dad, I boarded the plane which would take me to my connection point. More waiting, this time in the megalithic airport known as Charlotte, where I would board for the second leg of my journey back to Layton. Layton is not an easy place to access from distant points. At the gate for my plane, I recognized a good friend from my writers' group. A rush of joy and excitement always accompanies reunions in foreign and unexpected arenas.

"Cindy!" I yelled, and we hurried to embrace. Our mouths started clattering non-stop, and before we knew it, our wait time was over and our flight was boarding. Old hands at travel, we didn't rush the gate but relaxed to wait for our zones to be called.

The clattering and chattering continued and, somehow, we missed our zones. In fact, the door to our aircraft had closed. How did that happen without our knowledge? In unison and before a crowd of hundreds at ten conjoining gates, we banged on the closed door to the jet ramp. In hindsight, it was interesting that no security appeared to stop us.

Instead, the gate attendant showed up with a grin. "Why, girls, they had cake at the next gate, and I just had to get me some. You're OK. Here, I'll change your seats so you all can sit together." So, the chattering, clattering, and giggling continued on board until we reached Scranton where the sun rarely shines, but the friendship glistens.

Some days just shine, even when it's gray, and magical moments abound if we pay attention.

God just continues to lob joy-filled moments our way, but awareness of those moments is the result of time spent in God's presence, over His Word, and in prayer. Get to know Him. Understand the depth of love and sacrifice He has made for you, and as you live in an understanding of that, your sensitivity to His character and gifts will increase. Get to know God. In the discovery of His character, in the unveiling of His love for us, the world opens up in a miraculous way. Meet with Him daily on your road, and the cry of your heart will become, "Rejoice!"

Encouragement for Your Walk

"Rejoice in the Lord always, I will say it again Rejoice" (Philippians 4:4). Zero in on the beauty around you. Look for it. Try not to let a day go by on the road when you forget to rejoice in God's world, in His people, and in Him. Shiny days will become easier to find. Rejoice. Appreciation for God is the result of time spent together. Don't expect to overflow with daily joy if you haven't been learning of Him and talking to Him on a regular basis. Our Walk will shine the closer we draw to Him.

Lord, convict us daily to read and learn of you and to talk over the events of our lives with you. Calm our hearts and minds each day to see and enumerate the countless sources of joy around us for which we can rejoice. Teach us to rejoice in you always. Again we say, Rejoice.

40. The Best Medicine

Who among us couldn't use a little more laughter? Not only do our daily roads sometimes seem like drudgery, sometimes it's hard to find a reason to laugh, but laugh we must.

Bumps along the road of our walk leave us exhausted and weary. Sometimes a wild guffaw or a healthy laugh is good medicine for the soul. *"A cheerful heart is good medicine, but a crushed spirit dries up the bones"* (Proverbs 17:22).

One of my all-time favorite movie scenes involves laughter and an old actor named Ed Wynn as Uncle Albert in *Mary Poppins*. Singing "I Love to Laugh," he literally lifted off the floor and floated to the ceiling, light with the freedom of laughter. Bert (Dick VanDyke) and Jane and Michael Banks caught Uncle Albert's infectious laughter and drifted up to join him near the ceiling, all of them laughing uncontrollably as they tumbled and twisted, free from gravity and earth's bonds.

The characters in *Mary Poppins* each had his or her own share of difficulty and heartache. Bert was a poor chimney sweep, Uncle Albert lived the humble life of the aged, and Jane and Michael sought attention from their parents who were over-committed to work and personal interests and remained uninvolved in the children's lives. But from the ceiling of that sitting room, they all had a new perspective, and from those heights, they laughed, the laugh of the unfettered, the released, the free.

Every year, laden with illness, poverty, and war, brings a renewed need for perspective and laughter. Not the laughter of scorn or derision. Not a laughter of fools. There's plenty of that afoot. We need the laughter of joy.

For what's to be seen from the heights of our sitting rooms? Lives filled with small miracles. Grace running rampant on mundane days. Love in unexpected corners. The presence of the Eternal. God at work. Take a look around from up there, from a different perspective. See the joy of the forever-loved, the never-left-alone.

Those thousand-pound weights that bind our spirits to the floor, to the basement, even to the sewer, cling more tightly as we study them, contrive to escape them. Work to release the chains of anxiety. Take the perspective of God in eternity who encourages us to see the long journey's final destination and be cheerful.

But feel the freedom, experience the loosening of the bonds, watch the chain weights of worry fall as our perspectives shift—to the God who says, "Cast all your care upon me." Lay each weight at the foot of the cross and slap your spiritual hands each time you try to pick them up. He will carry the burden. His love and His power have already been proven on a cross.

Feel the weights fall off. Soar. Free. Up to the highest heights. Laughing the joy of the redeemed, the protected, the blessed, the forgiven, the loved.

Author Ann Voskamp calls this laughter "oxygenated grace." Author Anne Lamott calls it "carbonated holiness." Let's live high every day on the oxygenated, carbonated joy of our freedom and position in Christ. And let's laugh.

It seemed like a dream, too good to be true, writes the psalmist, *"when God returned Zion's exiles, freed from their bonds. We laughed, we sang, we couldn't believe our good fortune . . . God was wonderful to us; we are one happy people"* (Psalm 126:1-3, *The Message*).

Yes, we could use a little more laughter in the world and, certainly, here on Layton and perhaps on your street too.

Encouragement for Your Walk

"A happy heart makes the face cheerful, but heartache crushes the spirit" (Proverbs 15:13). Smile. Smile and mean it. Let a cheerful face invite smiles from others. Many days on our walk need smiles and all-out laughter. Ask God to help you see the humor and cheer in the journey's ordinary routine. Be quick to laugh at yourself and the situation. Watch a cat or a dog for a spell. Play with the under seven's for a few hours. Play a game like "Pictionary." How about a walk by a stream or through a pine forest—certainly, a smile awaits. Make friends with someone who has a healthy, God-honoring sense of humor. Seek joy in the moment.

Lord, give us your perspective on our lives so we can bask in the oxygenated grace and carbonated holiness of you. And, Lord, we could really use a good friend who makes us laugh.

Part 9
Future Generations

"When Enoch had lived 65 years, he became the father of Methuselah. After he became the father of Methuselah, Enoch walked faithfully with God 300 years ... Enoch walked faithfully with God; then he was no more, because God took him away."

Genesis 5:21-24

Six decades,
Walking his own directions,
Six decades,
Walking Enoch's way.
Then, on an Emmaus Road,
Enoch met God
In a new way,
As he had never seen Him before.
Emmaus-changed,
Enoch began a daily Walk,
A road of obedient following,
His own Layton Road in an ancient land.
And he walked—
Faithfully.
Faithfully,
Until he was no more.

Jo Ann Walczak

41. The Narrow Gate

Bertha and Beulah stretched—full length, beautiful specimens of porcine femininity, smooth, hairy skin across their burgeoning girth. In their undisturbed sleep, movement was labored and breathing heavy.

"Grab the hose. Maverick, get the foam soap," Wyatt yelled to his brother. "Let's get these ladies ready for the dance!" Sleep for Bertha and Beulah would be short-lived today. Their class would be called soon into the ring.

Disturbances to sweet slumber rattled pens around the barn as hoses, hay, and harried teens prepared their wards for the big show.

My grandsons, Wyatt and Mack, had been raising pigs or goats for about six years. Their entries this year, Bertha and Beulah, tipped the scales at several hundred pounds each. They looked lethargic and comatose in the pen, but the cold water hose roused the beast in them.

I make annual pilgrimages to the Harford Fair's pig and goat barns to enjoy the fun of the show. Pig barn living at the fair is not what I expected. My visions of pig barns were based solely on *Charlotte's Web* where sweet spider Charlotte goes to extreme lengths to make messages in her webs to keep her friend Wilbur from getting to the fair. Charlotte knew what Wilbur didn't know about his fate at fair's end. Her attempts to derail Wilbur's trip to the fair certainly weren't because of the accommodations. Bertha and Beulah and the thirty or so other pigs in the barn at the Harford Fair lounged in spotless, swept comfort.

The 4-H children at the fair who maintain the stalls and their animals do an immaculate job. The floors are thick with fresh hay, shoveled out regularly. The swine recline like hairy mountains, oblivious of the crowds about them, swishing their tails to ward off flies like fat dowagers on a Carolina veranda while emitting ear-splitting squeals if they happen to cross each other's personal space. The pens, decorated with posters for the competition, bear the name of the owner, the farm, the pigs' names, and the multi-colored ribbons indicating their prize position. *Feng shui* even in the pig pen. We congregate around the Gadsden Ridge Farm stall. It's family.

Most of the hogs who enter the show ring through the narrow gates are headed to the auction block by the end of the week to provide hundreds of pounds of chops, ribs, roasts, and bacon. And this would be the reason Charlotte sacrificed her life to save her friend Wilbur.

The real fun, the dance, is in the ring of the pig barn. The show is more interesting than most television sit-coms. Hosed down and shined up for their appearance before the judges, the pigs look worthy of a place in your kitchen, and the kids, likewise cleaned and spruced up, wear their best jeans, usually a plaid shirt, and sometimes a pair of boots that cost more than a Weber grill.

And bling is the thing—even in the pig barn. Many of the competitors, kids not pigs, wear wide Western belts embedded with turquoise, crystals, and colorful gems, and the four-inch-by-four-inch buckles are show-stoppers. Some girls wear flashy necklaces, drawing more attention to the showman than the pig, a good ploy if they have trouble controlling their wayward charges.

The plan is to walk your pig in a circle or a figure eight using a guide whip to gently tap the pig while simultaneously keeping your eyes on the judge with a smile on your face. Something like patting your head and rubbing your tummy at the same time—not so easy. The judge floats around the ring with a clipboard giving points to the showman for poise, posture, control, and personality and to the pig for shoulder width, leg distance, back length, and butt configuration. Muscle vs. fat becomes an issue to which both the hogs and I can relate.

Wyatt entered the ring through the narrow gate with Beulah. With strength and determination of their own, those pigs become a heavyweight challenge for the strongest-willed teenager once they enter the freedom of the ring. One pig heads for the exit shoot, another refuses to move, one skirts the edge declining to come out in the middle, another wants to run at break-neck speed, anywhere but here. It's a comedy of errors, and glory goes to the kid who can hold the judge's eye, direct his/her pig to the correct location, demonstrate control, and keep on smiling.

The judges award ribbons, and at the end of the event, the pigs leave the ring through the same narrow gate, pushing, shoving, squealing and squiggling.

The entrance to heaven is described in God's Word as a narrow gate, a metaphor for the difficulty following Christ may be for some people. After all, the broad way is peopled with the crowd, and it's easy to follow the crowd. Making the choice to follow Jesus puts us on a narrower road that requires sacrifice in our lives and taking on new patterns of life Jesus describes in the Sermon on the Mount—hard things requiring focus and commitment. But Jesus does not leave us alone when we accept His sacrifice for our sin, and we choose the narrow gate. He offers His power and the Helper, His Spirit.

Unlike the pigs, we get to make the choice to follow God's Way and avoid the final destruction. It's a narrow gate. The last thing we want to do is take a nap in the pig sty of life when the end looms

Encouragement for Your Walk

"Enter through the narrow gate. For wide is the gate and broad is the road that leads to destruction, and many enter through it, but small is the gate and narrow the road that leads to life and only a few find it" (Matthew 7:13-14).

Follow God's Way, the narrow gate, that leads to relationship with God and a home in heaven at the end of the road. The alternative? Choose the way of the world and stumble into the muck and mire lining the broad paths. Choosing wisely and well as we follow Him will change the landscape of our lives.

Lord, if any of my family or friends, if any of my readers, have not turned to Christ for forgiveness, open their eyes and their hearts to you and eternal life. Help them to choose the narrow gate and the road that leads to life.

42. Grabbing for Rings

"I want the white one," Sadee yelled as she headed toward a white pony with a pink saddle.

"I want one that goes up and down," Claire said as she climbed aboard a black beauty with teeth bared.

"I'm getting one on the edge because I want to grab for the rings!" Mack declared as he picked a noble-looking bay stallion.

We were on the Grand Carousel at Knoebels Amusement Park in Elysburg, PA.

The central attraction of our summer vacation for seven years was a trip to Knoebels for several days of camping and riding. My six grandkids have grown up a bit each summer on Knoebels' 1913 carousel, one of the largest in the world and voted #1 "Best of the Best" in amusement history by Golden Ticket Awards every year since the award's inception.

The children's all-day wrist bands allowed limitless rides, but the Carousel rider must get off after each ride and stand back in line. This gives everyone time to survey the herd again before choosing another steed from the stable of sixty-three handsome horses.

The Grand Carousel Organ sets the tone. The old pipe organ plays what has been called some of "the happiest music on earth," with clashing cymbals, beating drums, bells, and trumpets. Much of the music is from an era long before my grandchildren. It's Sousa and Goodman, not Gaga and Underwood.

As they've grown and taken on amusement park sophistication, the older grandkids have skipped the Carousel until later in their day and headed, first of all, to the Phoenix and the Twister to get their fill of roller coaster terror. But we have had a steady stream of younger children in the family who head directly to the center of the park and its *piece de resistance*, the park's *Grand Dame*, the Carousel. We've been to Disney World, and Walt certainly has created a massive entertainment kingdom, but the joy of Knoebels Park and the Grand Carousel are magnets for us.

One thing always draws the older ones back to the Carousel after they get their fill of hair-raising coasters: grabbing the rings.

To grab the brass rings, they have to sit on the outside rim of the merry-go-round. When the ride begins, a metal arm starts to dispense brass rings. The rider hopes the rise and fall of his horse will coincide with reaching the ring dispenser. There's a significant physical stretch involved as they lean precipitously off their horses. Sometimes they can grab the rings, and sometimes they grab air. The game is to see who can grab the largest number of rings. I've given up the reach for rings—too many variables that might leave me in an embarrassing position on the floor.

Every year when I choose my horse and begin the musical loops, I think about the metaphor of this classic amusement ride. For what rings am I reaching? Am I trying to give my life significance by grabbing for all kinds of rings?

Grabbing the brass ring is a cultural goal in America. We are on our horses and striving—for a bigger paycheck, a lake house, money, possessions, winter in the islands, name brand clothing, "bucket-list" experiences. Success is gauged by the rings we have accumulated. Grab what you can while still riding high. Don't fall off the merry-go-round. Aim to get more rings than the other game players. Those rings we've grabbed—are they an indicator of our significance, our purposeful lives, or our lasting satisfaction?

Exhausting. Fleeting. We're spinning endlessly, loop after loop of striving to put value in and on our lives. When in reality, it's all pretty temporary, a blink of the eye, passing pleasure, impermanence.

Is there one true brass ring for which we should be grabbing?

The Bible is clear: a relationship with the One True and Living God is the brass ring. Believe His promises. Abide daily in Him. Look to the good of others. Walk this life with His desires as the goal of life. This is eternity-lasting, brass-solid, unable to be tarnished significance.

Life's Grand Carousel of endless circling and grabbing can leave us empty and wanting. God's plan is for our eternal good, not for a temporary pacifier and amusement, a plan that will take us off the dizzying treadmill and galloping into personal fulfillment.

"Don't work for what spoils, but for what endures to eternal life, which Jesus gives . . . Believe in the One God has sent" (John 6:27-29).

This is God's Brass Ring.

Encouragement for Your Walk

Sometimes our Walk can become a treadmill with endless circling and grabbing for elusive, everchanging "brass rings." What brass rings are you chasing? Are you trying to maintain a status or persona? Endless circles, and within those circles, there are pressures—keep up with neighbors, push harder for promotions or better jobs, assure the kids have excellent school grades and excel, and on it goes. Circle, grab for the next ring. Who can grab the most? When the Walk gets dizzying, make a concerted effort to focus on God alone and the things that matter most to Him.

Lord, we are so easily distracted. Help us to walk with riveted attention on you and what you desire. Grant us wisdom and understanding to know what really matters in the bevy of choices we face each day. Help us to work for what never fails in your kingdom. Give us the courage to step off the Carousel and keep in step with your desires instead of the world's.

43. One-of-a-Kind Life

The triangular head of a viper disappeared behind a rock in its glass tank. A giraffe extended his tongue into a rain gutter to collect dead leaves. A cougar paced the perimeter of his enclosure. Prairie dogs darted in and out of holes. A lion tossed his mane and yawned a growl.

My grandchildren raced from cage to pen at the wilderness menagerie, squealing with fear and delight. Wyatt and Mack accompanied grandma to a local wild animal menagerie called Claws 'N' Paws Wild Animal Park for our annual "Back-to-School Bash." A spacious and natural park, shaded woodland trails, picnic tables, and outdoor enclosures for the animals filled the park. We often lunched at a table near some animal's natural habitat cage. Five-year-old Mack tended to stay close, but eight-year-old Wyatt kept a wary eye for places to run and hide.

Mistaking a fifty-year-old tortoise as a statue, Mack tried to climb on top. "He's alive!" Mack howled.

"He looks like your cat!" Wyatt exclaimed at the jaguar. An astute observation about the similarities in the cat family.

"Let's go back to the alligators," Wyatt shouted.

"Can we feed the parrots again?" Both boys had enjoyed the walk-in bird cage where exotic and colorful parrots alit on their heads, shoulders, or arms.

"Look at the chimpanzee swing!" said both boys as they followed the primates wild jumps, reels, climbs and antics around their enclosure.

Fur, scales, shells, feathers, necks, beaks, tails, horns. The zoo was a kaleidoscope of color, sound, and form. "Doesn't God have the most incredible imagination?" I asked the boys on the ride home.

"He sure does!" they agreed.

Truly, God's creativity as seen in animals defies comparison. Unique and varied, they are testimony to the wisdom of an omnipotent God who has more than one way to do something. And on our trip to the wild animal park, we viewed only a few of the thousands of animal species God created.

Remembering this should encourage our hearts in times of difficulty. God sees more than one way to create an animal and more than one way to approach a problem. We may see animals as strange or dangerous, but we can also look at them as magnificent creatures of God that fit into His Master Plan. God, in His creative, wise, out-of-the-box, neck-of-a-giraffe, trunk-of-an-elephant style, turns the impossible into the possible and opens a door when there seems to be no exit. God's wisdom, creativity, imagination, and love can be trusted to turn trials to victory.

Are troubles, heartaches, and temptations making your Walk a nightmare? Remember the cheetahs, tigers, lions, bears, and the thousands of animals on our planet who are examples of God's extraordinary imagination. Look to their Maker, and yours, and trust Him with your future for He has a unique plan for your one-of-a-kind life.

Encouragement for Your Walk

When danger stalks your Walk, remember, *"I am the LORD your God who takes hold of your right hand and says to you, 'Do not fear; I will help you'"* (Isaiah 41:13). When the road presents more problems, potholes, ruts and ditches than you think you can handle, remember your Creator God who has a million ways to do things. His imagination and ingenuity dwarf our plans. Tell Him the problem and trust Him to show you the right way. God's world abounds with billions of examples of His creativity. He knows the way through the problem. Seek answers and direction from Him.

Father God, today we lack courage and wisdom. We don't know what to do or which way to turn. Hold our hearts and our minds as we walk into that room or face the consequences of our actions or say goodbye. Give us your creative ideas, alternative actions, fresh ways to handle the situation. Help us to remember who you are. You will be our Helper, and You will deal with our problems in one of a million ways we can't even imagine.

44. Trudging with Excitement

Our annual family vacation at an amusement park would end in fifteen minutes when the park closed. As the crowd thinned, my grandchildren rode repetitively on their favorite rides as their all-day passes neared expiration. Three-year-old Mack had chosen his favorite, a John Deere tractor that circled behind a fire truck, a convertible, and a pick-up as they rotated round and round endlessly.

Even with the weariness of the day, his voice rang out in song as he revolved, the only passenger on the ride. His mom and I caught the garbled words and melody as he passed. "Riding my tractor. Farmer Andy mows the hay. Over the fields. Pull the wagon." The first vocabulary of his childhood featured farm life.

Early in the day, Mack's dad had taught him the thumbs-up signal. At first Mack had to study his hand to choose the correct digit before lifting it with a smile. Circling and singing on the John Deere tractor and the encouraging thumbs-up sign mastered, he gave us and the ride-operator a thumbs-up on every revolution. The ride-operator returned his smile with a grin of satisfaction. When someone finds joy in the routine and dizzying revolutions of their day, it inspires all of us to keep on going and not to become weary in the tedious nature of our lives.

Does life on your journey seem repetitive? Do your days become meaningless revolutions? Up at 5 a.m., pack lunches, kids off to school, off to work, home at 5 p.m., dinner, homework, laundry—repeat, repeat, the next day and the next? Drudgery. We encounter the same activities and the same people. We wonder about the purpose of all this ordinary repetition. Is life just a merry-go-round with no daily significance?

"Whoever can be trusted with very little can also be trusted with much, and whoever is dishonest with very little will also be dishonest with much" (Luke 16:10). Being faithful in small and routine jobs demonstrates faithfulness in larger works. Every routine is an opportunity to show our devotion to God. If we show ourselves faithful in the rising at 5 a.m., making lunches, completing good work on our job, and all of our other daily routines, we show ourselves to be trustworthy, faithful, and capable of larger goals. Our characters are displayed in the way we handle the minutia. We may need to "study our hand," like Mack, and work at it a bit to exercise our obedience, but a smile and a song of joy flow readily when we practice.

God has a plan and purpose for our lives, even though it may look less than glorious now and more like tedium. "Lord, show us today how you want to use us in your kingdom." He may tell you to help the new girl at work or labor through an entire geometry assignment with your son or watch a football game with your husband or leave an encouraging note for the garbage man.

Drudgery and routine can become purpose, but with each revolution or each passing day, even if we are circling alone, remember God's presence is constant, His promises are true.

Lift a thumbs-up of thanks at the end of each day to the sovereign Creator who smiles with satisfaction at our faithfulness to the task.

Encouragement for Your Walk

Character takes shape in the routine, the seemingly unimportant, the monotonous. *"… we know that suffering produces perseverance; perseverance, character; and character, hope"* (Romans 5:3-4). The endless circling of our days and the wearying sameness calls us to endurance. As we keep on faithfully doing our assigned tasks with a good attitude, character is nurtured and grown. Don't weary of it. Be thankful for it.

Others, like teachers, employers, and husbands, may notice your faithfulness even before you do. *"Let us not become weary in doing good, for at the proper time we will reap a harvest if we do not give up"* (Galatians 6:9). Every journey will witness the cessation of inner turmoil over the daily drudgery with the realization that these are my appointed tasks for the day, laborious and slogging as they may seem. God gave us these jobs and chores—reason enough to do the best we can.

Father, help us to go about our daily jobs with an attitude of enthusiasm. Give us the energy and the positive attitude to make a slog of a day into a slice of joy. Let a grateful heart and a contented spirit claim victory at the end of each of our days. Thank you for growing our characters in life's drudgery.

45. Shining Like a Star

My six-year-old granddaughter Claire dragged herself about the bedroom as the family prepared to attend the Christmas Eve church service. A *prima donna* who enjoys dressing up whether there is an occasion or not, Claire obviously didn't seem excited about the evening activity which would normally have her searching out her patent leather shoes, leopard sweater, and flouncy dress.

She and her sister Anna were to be characters in the church performance of the Christmas story. Anna had been assigned the part of an angel in the choir. Bedecked in her white robe decorated with tinsel and glitter, Anna was a vision in glitz.

Claire, on the other hand, was to be a sheep—one of four, all plain, brown and indecorous. No singing Christmas carols from heaven or flopping flashy wings for this little one. She just had to stand in front of the hay-filled box and look—sheepish. This was not Claire's style. "I want to be all sparkly!" She bemoaned her role in the play. "Like Anna."

You know, Claire, I want to be all sparkly, too. Who doesn't want to live each day shining? Unfortunately, I am also wrapped in plain, brown paper, Claire—a rather dirty, dismal farm animal, sometimes too dumb to get up when I fall over.

But I've learned an important lesson about sheep, my dear granddaughter. Not only has Jesus Christ forgiven us and washed us whiter than snow, the cleanest, most sparkling of whites, but He has given us a plan for shining.

We can sparkle even in the farmyard. We *can* "shine among them like stars in the sky" when we hold firmly to Jesus and His Word. It's the truth. Jesus says so in Philippians 2:14-15: *"Do everything without grumbling or arguing, so that you may become blameless and pure, children of God without fault in a warped and crooked generation Then you will shine among them like stars in the sky."*

Jesus compares us to sheep. He cares about every last one of us. In fact, He tells a story about a man who had one hundred sheep but one wandered off. Now the man had enough to do caring for the ninety-nine, but every last sheep carried great value to him. He left the ninety-nine to search for that precious, lost one. Claire, my little lamb, you are the precious one. That's how important you are as a sheep. When we come to Jesus and embrace His offer of love and sacrifice, the Bible says, He washes us whiter than snow—we shine.

Sweetie, we sheep *can* shine. Even if we spend every day of our lives in the muck of the farmyard, we can shine, sparkle, glitter—with Jesus. "Chin up, honey! You can always be sparkly for Jesus!"

Encouragement for Your Walk

Following Jesus shows great wisdom, and *"those who are wise will shine like the brightness of the heavens, and those who lead many to righteousness, like the stars for ever and ever"* (Daniel 12:3). God calls us to "shine," to be a light in this world who will bring Him glory by living a godly life. Right living does what is true, good, kind, and faithful. It is loving and wise living. It reflects the call God has put on our lives. Children, you will shine when you walk in the ways God asks. Shining—this is how we should live on the road.

Lord, we want to shine. We want to do good deeds, honoring you. We want to display love, joy, peace, patience, kindness, goodness, faithfulness, gentleness, and self-control. Help us to live wisely in your ways. Strengthen us to show these attitudes. Empower us by your Spirit for right living on our daily Walk—so we can shine every day.

Part 10
The Finish Line

"I have fought the good fight, I have finished the race, and I have remained faithful.

Acts 20:24

"But my life is worth nothing to me unless I use it for finishing the work assigned me by the Lord Jesus — the work of telling others the Good News about the wonderful grace of God."

2 Timothy 4:7

46. Locusts

"I will repay you for the years the locusts have eaten—
The great locust and the young locust, the other locusts and the locust swarm—
My great army I sent among you.
You will have plenty to eat until you are full,
and you will praise the name of the LORD your God, who has worked wonders
for you; never again will my people be shamed"
(Joel 2:25-26).

Eight-month-old Sadee nuzzles deep in my arms. With one hand she holds her fuzzy blanket. With the other she clutches my finger. Her eyes close, and I rub the soft down of her head and trace her forehead, her nose, and the soft fatness of her arms. Lifting her to my face, I inhale her powdery baby scent. Perhaps I should put her in the crib while she sleeps, but I don't. I cradle her for a two-hour nap. The dishes, laundry, and phone calls wait, unwashed and unanswered. Only holding Sadee matters as I drink in the joy of this child. Sadee leaves me breathless.

Cradling Sadee during her naps, I remember. Forty years ago on Mother's Day weekend, I cuddled Sadee's daddy Trevor after his birth. The same downy head, molded nose, and dimpled cheek. The same fresh, unsullied beauty.

Yet, in my bed on the hospital maternity ward all those years ago, I held my infant son and sobbed. Not for the sheer joy of this baby gift. Not for the blessing of a healthy child. I wept for his future and mine. A broken woman cradled a flawless baby, bathed in tears. The odds against us seemed monumental. What chance for this small one or his toddler brother? What would be required of the three of us seemed too much. The haunting threat of his father's desertion after the baby's birth loomed. I choked with fear, dreading impending disaster. Catastrophe followed quickly after his birth. I would parent solo—I was alone.

In the following days and weeks, a swarm of fears and worries began to encircle me—a horde, like desert locusts moving in to devour and destroy. My world turned black with their numbers. Advancing like an army, they hovered, poised to eat and leave me empty, engulfed in their darkness, swallowed in their gloom.

Locusts buzzed their messages. "Anyone who cares for you will eventually turn away. You are a disappointment as a wife and a mother." Locusts hummed louder, "Rejection. Failure. Grief. Guilt. Loss. Dashed dreams. Inadequacy. Not enough." And they multiplied: "Unloved. Unlovable. Shamed. Worthless. Fearful. Lonely. Not enough." I was eaten up from every direction. Locusts perched for an ongoing feast on my spirit and emotions. They would pursue me for years.

When locusts plague and paralyze your life, what is a woman to do? *How can God redeem a life from devastation?* I wondered. Like Pigpen in the Charlie Brown comics, a cloud of emotional dirt enveloped and trailed me, distorting my vision and hope.

Freedom from a blanket of darkness and locust infestation can only come from a Master Designer-Creator who knows plagues. I would learn that locusts take flight in the face of His presence and His love. God's lavish love for a broken woman rubs a salve of healing balm deep into the soul. It heals and clears the air. Brokenness is fertile ground for resurrection. God's love casts out rejection with acceptance and inadequacy with a totally sufficient Savior. It casts out failure with the divine victory of sacrifice, dashed dreams with hope for eternity. His love casts out shame with forgiveness, and loneliness with His everlasting presence.

But those realities would come slowly over the years. Healing is a process. God treats the broken woman with the gentleness of a gardener whose prize rose has been trampled and her petals plucked. Tenderly, He waters her with His promises: *"It is my desire to lavish my love on you"* (1 John

3:1). *"For I am your provider, and I meet all your needs"* (Matthew 6:31-33). *"My plan for your future has always been filled with hope"* (Jeremiah 29:11). *"I love you with an everlasting love"* (Jeremiah 31:3). The locusts begin to take flight as these whispers of love take hold of the broken one's heart.

The whispers continued on through the years: *"If you seek me with all your heart, you will find me"* (Deuteronomy 4:29). *"When you are brokenhearted, I am close to you"* (Psalm 34:18). And He led me closer to Him. From His promises came a new realization: My identity is in my relationship with Him, not in my rejection by someone else or by brokenness. I matter to God. I am His child and treasured possession and so are my children. He loves us even as He loved His Son, Jesus. He gave up everything He loved to gain our love. Nothing will ever separate us from Him.

Eventually, a plague-ridden woman could see the sky again. Hope was on the horizon.

Today, God assures me, *"I will repay you for the years the locusts have eaten . . . You will have plenty to eat until you are full, and you will praise the name of the Lord your God, who has worked wonders for you; never again will my people be shamed"* (Joel 2:25-27).

The locusts took flight. Shame was replaced with satisfaction in Jesus.

God's recompense for the years the locusts had eaten lies curled in my arms. I cuddle Sadee as she sleeps, the youngest of my six grandchildren, this precious grandbaby who, along with my five other grandbabies, is a second chance for joy.

Encouragement for Your Walk

Perhaps you, too, endure a difficult segment of your journey. Take it one step at a time. Left, right, left, right. Bit by bit. Always remembering, "I am God's. He is loving and faithful. He is here. He wants the best for me." Left, right, left, right. Slog on, when lifting your legs is burdensome, when raising your head seems impossible. Always remember, "I am God's. This is my identity, not what others say about me, not how I feel today about myself." Bad things, horrible thoughts haunt our Walk, but mindfully stick to the path. Left, right, left right. Remember who you are and who God is, as He leads and pursues you with a love that endures forever.

Almighty Father God, we are yours. A glorious end is assured because of Jesus. Help us to walk strong with the power of your Spirit until then. May each step we take, each mountain we climb, every valley we cross, be a growing, fruitful dependency on you. Left, right, left, right.

47. Tearing Down, Building Up

The little church on Layton near the Justus Corners was torn down a few years ago. The Scott Township Dive and Rescue, a division of the Justus Volunteer Fire Company specializing in rescuing drowning victims, contemplated its purchase as a storage base. Although they did not take ownership of the church, only God could orchestrate such a fitting reuse of the property. The church, in the business of saving people drowning in their sin, might have given way to another drowning rescue effort.

The lovely little church sat on Layton Road for over a century. Lovely might be a hyperbole, although well-meaning in intent, for she had fallen into disrepair.

Slatted shutters, some askew, all rotting, covered her windows against light and weather. Roaming critters found easy access through a few hidey holes. Weeds encircled the structure, blossoming in the rain gutters and climbing some walls to engulf her. Large field stones beside the front steps hiccupped out of place with the long winters. The white exterior turned to dishwater gray. The front door Kwikset lock was the only shiny new part of her wardrobe, but even this bolt couldn't hold off looters as a limp kick might cause the door's collapse.

Worst of all was the roof. The shingles jutted and curled in various directions, as if they wanted to take flight. The ultimate slap in her face and her final humiliation were the gaping holes in the roof, completing her progressive disintegration. A large pine tree landed on her in a storm a few years ago. She stood hurt and forlorn, taking on rain and snow. But even in her aloneness, she sat humbly, waiting to welcome someone within her walls. The bolt lock stayed secure. Her simplicity and stature veiled memories of covered dishes, picnics on the lawn, hymn sings, weddings, community friends, and a vibrant family life.

She was the Primitive Baptist Church of Justus, organized in 1835. Evidently, there are still a few members: three, according to one of the families who once belonged. They no longer meet anywhere on Sundays, or any day for that matter.

The one-room schoolhouse across the street, in use at the same time as the church beginning in the mid-nineteenth century, was also demolished in the last few years. Perhaps the fate of the little church was sealed, for she stood still and alone, one of the last vestiges of our village life in Justus. The older generation dies, the younger moves to Houston or Memphis, and the voices of happiness and love that once filled the place are muffled and finally silenced.

I liked giving the little church a good look every time I drove by or a nod or a thought about her days of singing and joy. She enjoyed the recognition. Glad to know she hadn't been forgotten.

Although it's only a quarter mile down the road from my home, it wasn't the church my family attended. We weren't Primitive Baptists. Our church, a half mile in the opposite direction on Layton, was "American" Baptist—whatever that meant and whatever the differences were between the two churches, I couldn't tell you. But some of my best friends went to the Primitive Baptist, and they were sterling family people. The little church bred them well.

Why, in this miniscule community, would we have two Baptist churches within a half mile of each other and no other denominations? I wonder if perhaps doctrine or theology or practice differed just enough between them in the mid-1800s to warrant two Baptist churches.

And that reminds me of the hole in the church. Could a difference in doctrine or practice be a hole? The hole in the roof of the Primitive Baptist was glaringly offensive, driving me to the "hole" in today's greater Church. For some people, perhaps the "hole" in today's Christian Church began with differences in doctrine and theology. Perhaps the "hole" in Church for some people is what they consider to be the hypocrisy of those who attend, or maybe it's what they consider to be the irrelevance of the church's message to the world in which they live. Or perhaps the "hole" in the Church for them is their opinion of churchgoers as judgmental or narrow. No doubt about it—the Church has "holes."

But, when it comes to holes, let's keep the focus: God.

God, the Creator, knows what and with whom He has to deal. He made us. He has a plan for us. He loves us in our messiness and divisions and hypocrisy and judgmentalism and humanness. Who else would? And the plan was for His own Son Jesus to take the punishment for all those things we do and have done that cause us to fall so short of His standards. I deserve no mercy, no grace, but God took that "hole" in my soul and did a miracle of healing with the blood of His Son Jesus.

God, the Lover of our souls, is the Promise Keeper, the Forgiver, Accepter, Redeemer of our lives—the Hole Healer. Don't let the holes you see in the church keep you from God.

Encouragement for Your Walk

And don't let the holes you have in your soul keep you from God. A hole in our souls, called sin, doesn't simply need repair. It requires a tearing down and rebuilding, possible only through God's forgiveness. Without it, a relationship and a Walk with God will be impossible. Confess those things, past and present, you know are separating you from God. His forgiveness mends the tears and makes all things new. No need to wallow in disrepair like the little church on Layton. Let God make you new. *"Therefore if anyone is in Christ, he is a new creation; old things have passed away; behold, all things have become new"* (2 Corinthians 5:17 KJV).

Lord, the burden of what we have done wrong, past and present, weighs heavy on our hearts along life's road. We have broken relationships, we have spoken harshly, not practiced kindness, glorified ourselves, neglected responsibilities. The burden of our sin is heavy. Help us to lay it down, to face the holes of sin in our lives and seek your grace, mercy, and forgiveness so we can walk with the assurance of your presence and love every step of our journey.

48. New Frontiers

Your Emmaus Road decision to follow Christ may seem like a century ago. You've followed His lead into mission fields, homeless shelters, churches, service of all types. The kids are raised. You've retired from your job. Now what? This may be the time to do something different.

Strange desires sometimes overtake us as we reach the far end of the road. Desires to do what we've never done, go where we've never been. Time is running short here on earth.

My father, by nature a man in search of new horizons, was on the prowl again. My mother warned me. Since she is not the adventuresome type, I often became my father's partner in risk or enterprise.

"I think I'll buy a sailboat," he explained excitedly, and before long a bright yellow boat with a boldly striped sail appeared in the back yard. My mother, with legs made only for *terra firma*, relinquished her right to be passenger on the maiden voyage to me.

That's how I came to be buckled and life-jacketed in the bow of our "Mayflower" at the boat dock of Lackawanna State Park. Naturally, the family all came along, expecting a good laugh, no doubt. My sister led the assembly with a movie camera, which was as novel to her as the boat was to us. A cheering crew, my boys ran up and down the dock, hoping to get in on the maiden voyage.

My sister's primary job was to hold the boat and the rope while my father readied the rudder and moved himself into position. Unfortunately, she let go, becoming too interested in the operation of the camera and the great shots this escapade would make. Fortunately, the boat stayed upright and refused to sail until my father's panic passed and the desire for adventure returned.

It was marvelous. The boat skittered lightly across the lake. The trees draped in full fall colors lined the water's edge, and we sailed, a small miracle. I was convinced that Dad had indeed conquered another new horizon when he commented that "John Paul" must have been among his ancestors since he also was of the "Jones" lineage, and that sailing had to be in his blood.

Unfortunately, the illusions went sour when he turned the sail and rudder from the "running with the wind" position, and the boat slowly slipped "John Paul" and crew into the cold of Lake Lackawanna. I suppose Dad failed to read the manual about turning into the wind.

My father had been awaiting this moment with the zeal of an admiral christening his first ship. Holding the rudder firmly in one hand, the sail rope in the other, and wearing a smile of satisfaction, a baseball hat, and his canvas tennis shoes, the captain went down with the ship—as did his one-woman crew.

Within minutes our buoyant boat was afloat again, but not without having taken on nearly three-fourths its capacity in water. Two drenched and shivering sailors maneuvered back across the lake—one wailing while the other used his tennis shoes to bail out the boat which now resembled an enlarged bathtub (minus the warm water).

Naturally, a crowd gathered at the boat dock to greet our arrival with much derisive laughter. Among them was my sister with the movie camera, preserving the sinking of John Paul for future generations.

The boat, the wind, and the captain could not agree on the correct angle for reaching our appointed landing place, so we sailed the coast, dragging along several fishing lines and bobbers in our rudder and dagger board while a few harried fishermen shouted obscenities to the wind (and the captain) about losing prized lures.

Finally, we decided to lower the sail and use an oar we kept aboard, just in case (a thoughtful birthday present to the captain from my sister).

Safely on shore, with not even a hand towel in sight, my father relaxed contentedly, the boat and the lake conquered. New frontiers open up no matter how old we are.

God often places dreams on our hearts, even in our golden years when the end of the road may be in sight. To many, those dreams may seem ludicrous and yet ... we feel that tug, that tap on our shoulder to come off our beaten path and pursue where God leads. At those times, putting our hope and trust in the One who knows our future will renew our aging strength. God satisfies the desires of the one who walks faithfully on the road of life with Jesus. Renewing our souls after a long, hard journey may require some interesting goals and projects.

"Praise the Lord, my soul...and forget not all His benefits—who satisfies your desires with good things so that your youth is renewed like the eagle's" (Psalm 103:2, 5). God satisfies the desires of the one who walks faithfully on the road of life with Jesus. A long, hard journey may mean some interesting goals and projects to renew our youth.

Encouragement for Your Walk

God fills our Walk with unplanned experiences and unexpected joys, gifts of encouragement propelling us on even when the waters are deep and our boat threatens to capsize. If God is prompting you to follow a turn in the road still headed in His direction, take the turn. You might find yourself teaching in China, leading a group of teen boys, starting a business, or even sailing a boat.

Lord, life often seems like serendipity to us but thank you for the plans You have for us, plans for hope and a future, plans to grow and change us. Thanks for the ongoing assurance of support and strength even in old age. Thank you for this promise: *"Even to your old age and gray hairs I am he. I am he who will sustain you. I have made you and I will carry you. I will sustain you and I will rescue you"* (Isaiah 46:4).

49. The Comfort of Song

One Easter morning, music brought my past to life and spoke to my loss and grief. You *can* hear your past, sometimes. I suppose circumstances have to be just right. But one Easter morning for me, they were, and my past literally sang a song of comfort.

The focus of Easter for our family has always been church. On Easter my family had an established routine that continued faithfully for about thirty years from the time I was an infant through my own child-rearing years.

Our family attended Mt. Bethel Baptist Church. Located only a quarter mile down the road from our home on Layton, it was the family place of worship from 1950 to 1980. Both sets of grandparents raised my mother and father in the church, too, taking our history with the church back to the 1930s. That's a family association with Mt. Bethel of fifty years.

But the church is much older than our family. Its history begins in the mid-1800s. Generations of farmers, miners, and laborers up here on the mountain have called Mt. Bethel, "House of God on the Mountain," their church. It's certainly old enough to have the ghosts of past congregants roaming about. In fact, as a child I mortally feared going into the church basement alone, a feeling solidified the time I encountered a black snake slithering through the old stone wall in the basement.

Mt. Bethel grew us. Our mothers and fathers carried us, shoved us, and pulled us there from the crib roll class to pre-school, then to youth group, until we walked the old burgundy and black carpet down the center aisle of the sanctuary to marry our sweethearts and, later, to bring our own babies to the crib roll class.

Carol, Jackie, Lynda, Sybil, Karen, and I were neighbors, schoolmates, and church chums. We came of age together. One Sunday night our small youth group was appointed to conduct the evening service. But our idols, the Beatles, were in America for their first appearance on the Ed Sullivan Show that night. We raced through the entire service, abbreviating the readings and songs (singing one verse only of the hymns, an unprecedented change of protocol), so we could get home to see the show. Our folks never let us forget the effect the Beatles had on our church. Mt. Bethel was family like that.

Grandpa Jones lived about six houses away from us on Layton. As church maintenance man, he would walk several times a week from his home to the church to do his chores. I'd see him pass the front window and run out to say hello. He didn't have a car in the 1960s, so he walked everywhere. On Sunday mornings he was the first one to get to church because he rang the bell, a large iron one in the steeple connected to a three-inch-wide rope in the church's vestibule. Each week as we entered the vestibule, there was Grandpa Jones, arms extended above his head, pulling with all his might. A short Welshman, I sometimes wondered how Grandpa wasn't lifted off the floor and flung to the belfry. The bell could be heard all over the top of this mountain and up and down Layton. Churchgoer or not, everyone received a call to worship.

And when we worshipped, we always sat in the same pew. It wasn't assigned. We hadn't paid for it. It was simply the Jones pew on the left as we entered the sanctuary, second row from the rear. Grandpa Jones always sat on the end of the pew by the center aisle, convenient for fixing the thermostat, shoveling the front stoop, helping Mrs. Sarnoski to her pew, or whatever. Next to him sat Nana Jones who never came to church without a hat. I liked sitting next to her. She had soft jiggly excess layers on her upper arms we children liked to wiggle. Then mom, one or both of my sisters, and dad sat on the far end of the pew. Dad and Grandpa bookended our pew with all us Joneses in between. When my boys came along, they fought to sit by Pa, my dad, who enjoyed their presence but not their folderol in church. We would often have to drag their escaping bodies from under the pews.

The Jones pew could sing. Grandpa, a miner who immigrated from North Wales in the 1920s, stood about five-feet-five-inches but carried a powerful tenor voice, groomed in the best Welsh tradition in the pubs and chapels of the old country. I can still see his white wisp of hair, round wire-rimmed glasses, and well-worn suit and silk tie. His strong tenor belied his size, and his voice, easily identifiable in a room full of strong singers, would have made any *Gamanfa Ganu* proud.

On the right side of the church sat the Evans and Morcom families, also in their designated pews. Both Jack Evans and Albert Morcom maintained an equally high volume although without the pitch perfect voices of the Jones family, so the Joneses said. Jack's trump card was his wife Janet who sang alto. She carried all of us in the church who couldn't hit the high notes with my mother. Mom and Janet had been singing duets since they were teens. Left side versus right side of the church, a singing competition raged every Sunday morning. Our post-church dinner conversations usually alluded to the volume or key of the morning's hymns.

The climax of our singing year at church was Easter. "He Lives, He Lives! Christ Jesus Lives Today!" could be heard at Justus Corners, a mile away, followed by a more mellow "In the Garden." We managed a rather vociferous "And He walks with me and He talks with me, and He tells me I am His own." But the *piece de resistance* was "The Old Rugged Cross." Every man, woman, and child in the place sang it with gusto and sincerity.

The singing began at about 6 a.m. every Easter morning. Sunrise service was standard protocol, followed by a full breakfast of pancakes and eggs in the back of the church. Jim Carpenter was usually the cook *extraordinaire* and supervisor in the kitchen. Jim, our cigar smoking Sunday School teacher, always had the kids' attention as he was a master of "stealing noses."

After breakfast we children would be eager to get home and find our Easter baskets. Mom would hurry us into our new dresses with matching hats, white gloves, and shiny shoes. Dad would present each of us with a small corsage, and off we'd go to church again to sing those same precious songs we'd sung at six—but that had only been rehearsal. At the 10 a.m. service we were warmed up, tuned up, and ready to raise the rafters.

And so it went, year after year. Eventually, I left the little church down the road. People change. Life moves on. Although I left Mt. Bethel in the 1980s, in recent years I've been back to buy Welsh cookies or to attend funerals. There have been quite a few, both cookies and funerals: Grandpa and Nana Jones, Mom, Dad, my friends Carol, Karen, Sybil, and Lynda, Jack and Janet Evans, Jim Carpenter, Albert Morcom, and the rest, right and left sides of the center aisle. A few years ago, Mom's funeral was at Mt. Bethel even though she had been living the retired life in Myrtle Beach for thirty years. At the funeral we played a tape of her and Dad singing the old hymns together. When Dad died, the service ended with a video of him playing his guitar and singing "Beyond the Sunset."

The iron bell in the steeple belfry has been silent for a long time. In fact, the bell may be gone. But the little church down Layton hasn't left me.

During Easter week one recent year, I passed Mt. Bethel's outdoor bulletin board: "Sunrise Service 6:30 a.m. Easter Morning. Breakfast afterwards." That's all it took.

By 6:25 a.m. on Easter morning, I entered the front doors of Mt. Bethel and noted the absence of the dangling belfry rope . . . and the absence of Grandpa Jones. This time my attendance wasn't for a funeral; it was for a resurrection, and Jesus had called me home to remember the power and beauty of His sacrificial love. I took my assigned seat, left side, second pew from the rear. About thirty people eventually filtered in, but I only knew two in the entire congregation. And then we started to sing . . . the same old hymns I'd been raised on all those Easter mornings ago. But a strange thing happened.

I heard Grandpa's strong tenor as we launched into "He Lives." I heard Mom's soprano hitting the high notes none of us could reach, Jack's toneless gusto, Albert's volume, and Dad's harmonization with Mom. The church resounded with their voices. I heard them all, just as if it were 1960 with the place alit and abuzz with people I loved on our most precious holiday.

You *can* hear the music of your past, and sometimes . . . if you listen carefully, it will sing to you, soothing the aches and griefs of a dusty journey.

"Music washes away from the soul the dust of everyday life," wrote German writer Berthold Auerbach. Author Victor Hugo concurred: "Music expresses that which cannot be said and on which it is impossible to be silent."

The Walk toward eternity accumulates plenty of dust and dirt. Sin and scum have a way of sticking. Prayer and confession are the most effective cleansing agents for the clinging crud of life, but God-honoring music, like aloe for sore feet, soothes and comforts and expresses the deepest needs and cries of our hearts. God-honoring music has a place of importance on your Walk. God rejoices over us with singing. Walk closely with Him and listen.

Encouragement for Your Walk

When King Saul, wracked by an evil spirit and entrenched in sin, could not rest or sleep, a servant suggested calming music. The servant knew of David's musical prowess on the lyre, so Saul invited David to his court. When an evil spirit came upon Saul, he would seek relief through David's music and *"he would feel better"* (1 Samuel 16:23).

When distractions abound and troubles roll ceaselessly, move off the beaten way. Sit. Talk to God and listen for His quiet voice and music from His heart. Listen. *"Be still and know that I am God"* (Psalm 46:10).

Father of our generations, we mourn the loss of those we love. We look back on the road behind, and we grieve for them. Keep us focused on you, on the unfolding world ahead of us, on continuing to step into the future and glory with you. Play your music to our hearts. Help us to hear your songs of love over us.

50. The Waiting Room

Kelly Ripa announced her next guest from the corner television. Other than Kelly and her husband Mark's banter on the screen, the waiting room lay silent. Every chair's occupant glanced blankly at the screen without reaction to the guests' humorous stories or the audience's laughter. Some looked at their hands or their phones or the curtain separating them from the adjoining areas. Conversation seemed superfluous, except when a woman entered the crowded waiting room, and a gentleman rose to offer his seat. Weighty thoughts took precedence.

Every few minutes, a technician or nurse would enter the waiting room from the adjoining area and call someone by their first name, an effort to personalize the impersonal, and summon them to the radiation room.

Waiting for my name to be called, I attempted conversation. The silence weighed too heavy. I queried someone, "Where are you from? How long have you been coming here?" And then the elephant-in-the-room question, "What kind of cancer do you have?" Perhaps the question seems more intrusive than necessary, but it was no secret: everyone in the waiting room had cancer.

With the question out there, the silence cracked. Eager to tell their stories, descriptions of cancer discovery and treatment flowed. What doctor? Chemotherapy? How many radiation treatments? Retelling rubbed a balm into wounded hearts—"someone wants to hear my pain. This too can be shared." Retelling helps. Let them talk.

THE WALK ON LAYTON

Esophageal cancer, lung cancer, colon cancer, liver cancer, a mixed bag of the worst killers inhabited the silent sufferers around the room. Conversations each day revealed their stories. With my early-stage breast cancer, I felt unfit to sit among these noble mortally wounded.

"Jo Ann?" The nurse at the curtain called my name as she had done for the past fifteen days. Conversation with others in the waiting room stopped. We exchanged, "Good luck, God bless, get well." Their sincere wishes followed me through the door—as if the grave were up ahead. This group knew the immediacy of the grave and the reality of life's "waiting room."

Preparation for radiation and the killing of cancer cells followed a pattern. Strip to the waist, lie on a table, arms stabilized above the head. I shuddered with apprehension yet again and with the cold of the room. The two friendly, young technicians situated my body and warned me not to move. They lined up their machine to the small tattoo marks made on my chest weeks before which indicated the radiation target. Then, they left the room through the six-inch thick door, and I was alone. No family member or friend to speak encouragement. No doctor or nurse to warn of the next step or to ask if I was alright. Alone.

Perhaps much of my life had prepared me for these radiation treatments and cancer.

From my first encounter with Jesus on my Emmaus Road forty-six years before when the Layton Walk began, God had spoken His truths over and over into my mind and heart. When my husband rejected me, He said, "Be strong and of good courage. Be not afraid. I am with you wherever you go." When my children struggled to grow up under the leadership of an inadequate single mom, I heard, "I will never leave or forsake you." Over and over facing junior high and high school students and the apprehension it often aroused, His voice never failed, "I am here," yes, even in the public school. During the year in China without my family, "The Lord is with you wherever you go," sounded in my soul. God's Spirit never let me forget it. The beauty of it echoes encouragement and strength.

The radiation machine moved slowly right to left above my body. It stopped. A red light as sharp as a laser shone down, perhaps pinpointing the alien cells. A buzz began. I knew it was the shooter, the power of radiation to kill. The buzz ended, and the machine encircled my body again, left to right. The red laser light focused. The buzz began. And the buzz of God's reminder never stopped humming. In His steadfast love and faithfulness, He whispered to my soul, "You are mine. I am here. You are safe in my care. Cast your fears on me. I will never leave or forsake you."

From Emmaus to this radiation day, my Walk had covered almost five decades—a slow slog of falling and getting back up, of veering off His path and coming back, of thinking I had utterly failed in my journey and then rejoicing because God refocused my attention on Him and His will for my life. The Walk continues as He renews my youth and sustains me in my old age. His hand before me and behind me, and His right hand above me.

Encouragement for Your Walk

On the Layton Walk, God's unfailing love has led the woman He redeemed in our encounter on that distant Emmaus Road. The reality and truth of 2 Timothy 1:12 became a developing assurance as the years passed: *"… I know whom I have believed and am convinced that he is able to guard what I have entrusted to him until that day."* Through the decades, He has shown me His love, mercy, kindness, and faithfulness. He has persuaded this stumbling pilgrim that He is able to encompass me in the beauty of who He is until that day when I am Home.

Father God, thank you for reaching out your hand of love to my readers. Give them clarity and strength to make an Emmaus Road decision to walk with you. Help them to see and hear the blessings of your forgiveness and grace. Empower them to keep seeking you and following you on their Layton Road through life. Amen.

51. The House on Layton

We've been together a long time, this old house and I on Layton … a lifetime for me. My Layton Walk with God launches daily out of its homebase and epicenter in this old house. But the house flexed its first muscle long before I was born.

Grandpa Evans built this two-story, box-style in the early 1930s with the help of Uncle Cliff, Uncle Dave, Uncle Walter, Uncle Gordy, Uncle George, and Uncle Vic, Grandpa's brothers-in-law. They hand dug the house's basement and well, not an unusual piece of work for this cadre of coal miners. A rock ledge hampered the work as surely as the economy of the Depression, but this group of brothers-in-law from North Scranton made it a family effort with a bit of dynamite, a tool often used during their coal mining years.

They built the house with three rooms down, three rooms up, and a 45-degree angle on the roof. The only bathroom, located on the first floor near the kitchen, had the family bathing and then running upstairs to the bedrooms—for the next thirty years. Closets were non-existent downstairs, a problem that took that same thirty years to correct. Lathe and plaster walls, yellow pine floors throughout, arched doorways, five-inch moldings, and hundreds of pounds of hot water radiators still grace the house.

Dad took over home maintenance when Grandpa Evans passed. Like Grandpa, he proved to be a master craftsman. Dad built a house for his family right next door to Grandpa's, and he and Mom raised their three daughters there. My years were spent back and forth daily between the two houses on Layton.

The generations rolled on: Grandpa and Nana Evans died, then Mom and Dad retired to South Carolina. My sisters moved out of town and out of state, and I—I stayed on Layton in Grandpa's house. My sons grew up romping through the same rooms as my sisters and me and my mother before. And now my grandchildren use the same hiding places and ride their bikes in the same route around the yard.

The front door of Grandpa Evans' house has welcomed five generations of our family. Originally accessed by a few wooden steps, the front door eventually gave way to a small concrete "stoop" which later expanded to a roofed porch that ballooned to a deck in its seventieth year. And the front porch of this old house has seen its share of family moments.

Take that day back in 1940 when my mother stood there waving goodbye to her sweetheart with no certainty of his sure return. The sweetheart, who would one day be my dad, came to the house for one last kiss as he shipped out to destinations unknown. All hell was set to break loose around the world, not just in my mother's heart. Dad would spend World War II in foxholes throughout North Africa, Sicily, and Italy for five years. Imagine the reunion on this old porch in 1945 when that handsome soldier marched up the steps and took his wartime sweetie in his arms.

Then there was the time in the late 1930s when cousin Ida Mae Reid took her first look at the world outside from this old porch. Aunt Millie came to stay with her sister, Nana Evans, here in the house on Layton while her husband, Uncle Cliff, built a home for them right next door. Aunt Millie was eight months pregnant. In those days many infant deliveries occurred at home, and that's what happened. Aunt Millie gave birth in the room off the kitchen which I now use as my dining room.

The little girl, Ida Mae, born a bit small, was bundled up by her aunts in warm cotton and shoved in the oven. Yes, the oven. This homemade incubator kept the little one warm, not baked, until she grew big enough to be carried out on the porch for a look about. Ida Mae is now in her eighties and retired in Florida (perhaps the oven incubator predisposed her to warm temperatures). Nevertheless, she is no worse for the wear because of her beginnings in General Electric's finest.

In 1950, Grandpa Evans had a heart attack on the cellar steps. His viewing was held in the living room before he, too, left this house for the last time.

I've stood on the porch for a few final goodbyes. Nana Evans died in that same room off the kitchen. I spent the last week of her life sitting beside her there. I watched as the undertaker carried her out the front door in a black bag, leaving for the last time the house that she and my grandfather had built.

Thirty-four years later, I stood on the porch, holding the door again for another final goodbye. The EMT's carried Mom out the door and into the ambulance after her fatal stroke.

Two generations slipped off this earthly sod through that door on our old porch.

As much as I miss my mother and grandparents, I am grateful that the next door they entered, after leaving our family home, opened to a mansion, not on Layton, but on a street of gold, in their heavenly forever home.

Then, I watched my husband walk out that same door. And my journey on Emmaus and then my Walk on Layton led to forgiveness, peace and finally, joy, as we grandparent the six children of our next generation. My soul finds rest.

Five generations have opened the door, slammed the door, let the cat in, let the dog out, posed for graduation photos, carried suitcases and boxes off to college, squeezed wedding gowns through the portal, bundled in new babies, and heard, "Don't stand there with the door open! You're letting the flies in!"

Yes, the door on this old porch has witnessed its share of comings and goings ... and will hopefully see many more.

Encouragement for Your Walk

"Remember how the Lord your God led you all the way in the wilderness these forty years, to humble and test you in order to know what was in your heart, whether or not

you would keep his commands" (Deuteronomy 8:2).

Remember: a godly mindset of gratefulness that rehearses the love and kindness of God through the years brings joy and hope. Look what God has done. See how each event of the past brought you into a closer relationship with Him. We can find hope as past events reveal God's hand directing, leading, and blessing us.

Thank you, Lord, for our history, for our generations, friends and past events. You have used their godly wisdom to guide and bless our lives. Thank you for this old house on Layton whose roof and walls and love have sheltered my family, and thank you for this old body, a dwelling of a different sort, that houses your Spirit and a heart eager to walk with you.

52. A Moment in Time

May our Walk bring significance to our Moment.
May we live each second of our Moment for Your pleasure.
May Your light shine unimpeded here
And be a guide in the darkness.
On our Walk, may You be worshipped, lifted, honored.
Use each second in our Moment for Your glory.
When our Moment in Time ends,
And the road we've walked vanishes,
Enclose us in Yourself, on the final part of our journey,
Hold us tightly for
Home is in sight.
Our Moment finished.
Our Walk complete.

Acknowledgments

My sincere and loving appreciation …

To Michele Chynoweth, a first-class editor and new friend, who walked patiently and gently with me through this book. Thank you for suggestions and changes that transformed my family legacy gift. Thank you for helping to make a life goal a reality.

Thanks also to Terri Velardi for conversations about publishing that sorted out a jumble of random ideas.

Many thanks to Robin Axtell for his beautiful cover design, to Caitlyn Arden Photography for my author photos, and with special appreciation to Tom and Fran Novitsky for the cover photo of Layton Road portraying the beloved Novitsky family farm.

To my first and only writers' group: Sherry Boykin, Leslee Clapp, Barb Engle, Becky Loescher, Gail Mills, Cindy Noonan, and Sarah Phillips. Your enthusiasm for writing, ideas, styles, and Scripture fostered my love for words and stories. Your dedication held me accountable. Your friendship cultivated our sisterhood bond around writing, the Scripture, and Jesus. Together we witnessed Sarah's godly Walk until she reached Home. You have penned the very best stories—without ink.

To the "Bookies." You have kept my heart and mind awash in good, bad, and challenging books. Thanks for motivating discussions, interesting meetings, and friendship. Thanks for keeping our aging minds sharp and our hearts open: Arline Drann, Colette Hughes, Sue Keisling, Paula Love, and Betty Walczak.

For faithful and encouraging friendships. At some point through the decades, your kindness and sensitivity strengthened and inspired me. You have exemplified godly lives and set the bar for friendships very high. Often, you have been the impetus and motivation for taking the next step on my Walk. You have lovingly journeyed some difficult roads with me. Thank you: Linnea Brown, Paul and Lisa Bell, Sharon Briggs, Marsha Evans, John and Lois Gilchrist, Gail Haggerty, Donna Imel, Al and Sue Keisling, Mark and Sue Lombardi, Kathy Roper, Elaine and Carolyn Saar, Dorothy Sewell, Barb Siniawa-Costello, Jim and Corinne Sohns, Tony Spears, Linda Specht, Bob and Nancy Stephenson, Marilyn Stracham, Bob and Sandi Thomas, Betty Walczak, Pat Walters, Steve Ward and Gao Yun.

To my Lakeland High buddies. Your laughter and companionship invigorated my teaching days as we helped each other get through some tough stuff. Thank you: Brad Bowerman, Al Chelik, Paula Love, Janice Marcks, Linda McClave, Karen O'Connor, Ann Marie Salitsky, Frank Santoro, Linda Stephens.

To the women in my Bible study groups for the past two decades at Parker Hill Community Church and LCBC. Your desire to know Christ and follow His lead has inspired me. You have been "My Church on the Walk," studying and growing together, standing with each other as life battered our daily living, sharing, praying, helping. Forever grateful to my small group: Rebecca Banik, Carissa Butler, Jeanne Corey, Cindy Davis, Bonnie Dodd, Judy Hughes, Diane Keller, Jane Lenz, Grace Lines, Carrie Lydon, Heidi Marion, Barb McGary, Tara Mielo, Laura Nathans, Alex Roe, Michelle Roshan, Liz Sandrowicz, Dorothy Sewell, Terri Velardi, Brenda Young, Judy Youshock, Zoe Godfrey.

To the Scott High School Class of 1966 who have been steadfast friends for seventy years and have entrusted me with special love and responsibilities. You have defined faithfulness and peopled some of my best memories.

To my sisters and brothers: Sally and Bob Corrigan, Nancy and Scott Reichert and their children who form our "family circle" around our Layton Road table for every holiday and major event, in the yard for picnics and badminton, even a hospital homecoming, a faithful support net: Shayna, Mike, and Jacqueline Mark; Zach Reichert and Ailsa Wood;

Garrett Reichert; and the Corrigan clan.

To Mom and Dad, Joseph and Annette Jones, for living unconditional love to my sisters, me, their grandchildren and great-grandchildren, and for providing my forever example of forgiveness, parental nurture, unfailing and graceful love, work ethic, strength for daily living, and devotion to God and family. You gave us girls a powerful start and an ongoing commitment, and you stepped into the lives of my sons to give the same unconditional love, helping to cover bases for this single mom. Dad read most of this manuscript before his death and, in his typical encouraging way, said, "Now, you finish this, Jo." Here it is, Dad. I hope it honors you and our Heavenly Father.

To my sons, Bryan and Trevor Walczak. Survivors of a clueless single mom, you blossomed, despite it all, into strong, hard-working, responsible, intelligent, thoughtful, sensitive, and kind men. Truly, you are the result of God's watch care, help, and endless mercy and grace through the years. You were the reason God gave me to keep going in difficulties, to put one foot in front of the other in heartache. You have enriched and blessed my life beyond measure. Grateful for the gift of you.

And thank you for bringing into our lives, your beautiful, intelligent, and talented wives, Janine and Casie. Girls, I admire your hard work, creativity, energy and devotion to your families. I am so grateful for all you have brought to our family.

Thank you, Bryan and Janine, Trevor and Casie, for a marvelous roundup of spectacular grandchildren, who, like you, are the heartbeat of all of our days: Ben, Anna, Claire, Wyatt, Maverick, and Kassadee—the Walczak tribe, my generations. Your Mama Jo/YiYo thinks each one of you is incredible in countless ways. I love all the moments we spend together. Forever your cheerleader, forever your friend. Thank you for bringing beauty and love to my Walk. You are the best.

To God, my ever-present Redeemer who, in His mercy and grace, has faithfully walked every step of the journey with me and my loved ones here on Layton and everywhere. Lord our God, you are worthy to receive glory and honor and power.

About the Author

Jo Ann Jones Walczak has lived most of her life on Layton Road in Northeastern Pennsylvania. Teaching junior high English and high school journalism for thirty years gave her a powerful mission. A single mom of two sons, she raised her boys on family, faith, and camping, traveling with them to almost every national park in the United States with a Coleman two-burner and a pup tent. When the boys were grown, Jo Ann set off across the world to teach for a year in China. She returned there several times to work in an orphanage. Leading Bible studies for women in her church—and now writing this, her debut book—has been her passion. Time with her six grandchildren is her greatest joy.

Contact the Author at:
Joannjoneswalczak.blogspot.com

www.ingramcontent.com/pod-product-compliance
Lightning Source LLC
Chambersburg PA
CBHW050726010526
44107CB00009B/748